MW01139078

Praise for *Safe to Great*

"Exceedingly entertaining and compelling, *Safe to Great* leaves the reader engaged and thinking deeply as to how best to face our challenges—both individually and collectively as a planet. I look forward to adopting the models and principles Bowman shares here throughout my organizations."

CHARLIE PILLANS, CEO and Entrepreneur, UK

"The principles in Skip Bowman's *Safe to Great* have formed the foundation for the leadership and culture at the Northern European region at Danfoss. In *Safe to Great*, Skip supplies you with comprehensive yet easy-to-understand insights and tools to identify behaviors, form a strategy, and create impactful change. I highly recommend this book to all leaders no matter level or seniority. It's never too late to learn."

SANDRA BERTELSEN, Regional Head of HR, Scandinavia, Danfoss

"*Safe to Great* is changing the game for leadership development. It represents a shift in the leadership paradigm and provides a new lens for leaders to see themselves and the organizations they lead. This book is genuine, effective, and engaging, and promises to create a deep impact with leaders at all levels. This book made me pause, reflect, and commit to being a leader who is not afraid to walk down the road less traveled and be courageous in my choices."

SWATI SETH, Senior HR Director, EMEAI, MKS Instruments

"Skip Bowman's book *Safe to Great* is both confrontational as it is inspirational. It clearly explains how organizations where people feel psychologically safe can adapt a growth mindset. Bowman points out how confrontational leadership behaviors negatively influence performance, and how, by adapting a growth mindset, leaders can inspire change in their organizations so they can adapt to and survive in today's ever changing business environment."

JAN SCHOEMAKER, Regional President, Asia Pacific Region, Danfoss

"*Safe to Great* goes beyond the "why?" of great leadership and into the "why now?!" Bowman ingeniously synthesizes our daunting and unprecedented global context and incites a call to action that embraces the challenges, responsibilities, and opportunities for leaders in today's world. Skip's unique use of metaphors and his ability to communicate complexity in a succinct and catchy way makes learning from his extensive experience with leaders, their teams, and his leadership research, compelling and impactful."

CHRISTINE KHALIFA,
Independent Leadership Consultant, South Korea

"*Safe to Great* is extremely engaging and connects growth mindset development to leadership agility within organizations. The examples and cases Bowman describes are very interesting and the hippo metaphor and character are unforgettable."

TOM SEBASTIAN, Co-Founder & Program Director,
NORDIN SME Accelerator, India

SKIP BOWMAN

SAFE TO

The New Psychology
of Leadership

GREAT

Vancouver / Toronto / Berkeley

23 24 25 26 27 5 4 3 2

Cataloguing data is available from Library and Archives Canada.

ISBN 978-1-77327-230-6 (hbk.)
ISBN 978-1-77327-231-3 (ebook)
ISBN 978-1-77327-239-9 (audio)

Author photograph and illustrations by Justyna S.

Editing by Lesley Cameron
Proofreading by Renate Preuss
Indexing by Stephen Ullstrom
Printed and distributed by Ingram

Figure 1 Publishing Inc.
Vancouver BC Canada
www.figure1publishing.com

Figure 1 Publishing is located in the traditional, unceded territory of the xʷməθkʷəy̓əm (Musqueam), Sḵwx̱wú7mesh (Squamish), and səlilwətaɬ (Tsleil-Waututh) peoples.

To my children, Joey (Eric), Mathilde, Sienna, Zoe, and Milou. Read this book some day. It might explain what your dad was doing all that time when he wasn't with you.

To my parents, June Cruickshank and Brian Bowman, whose gifts and imperfections got me started on a journey to work out what life is really all about.

To my brothers, Kyle (Geoffrey) and Peter Bowman. Yes, despite the wisdom in this book, I'm still your bossy little brother.

Contents

Foreword

IN MY EARLY TWENTIES, I landed my first professional role as a budget analyst in a mid-sized New England city. City Hall was a rough and tumble environment where strength, political cunning, and a certain facility with profanity were valued. No delicate flower, I was, however, inexperienced, and naïve. And as the first woman to be hired into the budget office, I felt conspicuous and self-conscious.

A few months after I started, my manager, Marty, pulled me aside to tell me he'd hired another woman into an analyst role. That was the good news. The bad news, delivered without explanation, was that she'd been hired at a grade level above me, *and* I was to turn most of my assignments over to her, after briefing her on the content of each task. I assumed the new analyst had done a better job than I had negotiating her entry into the organization. And because I seemed compliant, well, my needs were immaterial.

This happened late on a Friday afternoon, which gave me the weekend to move through the hurt and anger and consider my options. Confronted with the choice to be silent or speak up, I realized I'd have to overcome both my need for approval and my fear of conflict. Mind you, at that time there were few guides on how to have difficult conversations or deal with a problematic manager. And if you'd told me I would spend decades coaching, teaching, and writing about these and other leadership challenges, I would have been astonished.

On Monday morning I headed to Marty's office. Red-faced and nervous, but resolute, I sat down, uninvited. The conversation was brief. I looked Marty directly in the eye and said, slowly and emphatically, "I *want* a promotion." "Yes, yes," Marty said, nodding vigorously. Clearly I had caught him off guard; but he knew full well "he'd done me wrong." He didn't even try to justify himself. I paused. "I want it *now*," I said.

Three weeks later, I had my promotion in hand. And not coincidentally, Marty and I went on to develop a respectful and productive relationship.

That single encounter taught me a lot about bullies, blind spots, and belief systems. It is learning that has served me well in my leadership journey. In the decades since, I've come to see that most of us enter the world of work ill-equipped to lead, gripped by internalized fears and assumptions. Meanwhile, the leadership industry has mushroomed, pumping out largely simplistic formulas that glorify the heroic leader. As Barbara Kellerman reminds us in *Bad Leadership*, leadership isn't always good; in fact it's often bad—a reality that's become more obvious in recent years.

The central issue that *Safe to Great* tackles with insight and humor is that organizations are living systems, made up of complex beings with multiple identities and sometimes contradictory assumptions and beliefs. In today's world, these concerns are magnified as we adapt new work practices following the seismic disruption of a global quarantine. What is called for are purposeful and imaginative responses, and facilitative leadership, to foster our best collective thinking about the problems at hand.

In her seminal book, *Dignity: Its Essential Role in Resolving Conflict,* Donna Hicks integrates recent findings across multiple fields to shed light on these day-to-day challenges. Dignity, Hicks argues, is the need to feel valued and worthy. When that need is met, we experience genuine connection. On the other hand, dignity violations—such as lashing out or gossiping—trigger our limbic systems, and we are flooded with feelings of humiliation. We are ashamed of our own shame, and therefore deny it, instinctively protecting ourselves. Yet our brains are also equipped with a powerful ability to connect and feel empathy for others. It is this capacity to create meaningful connections that grants us dignity, that helps us feel safe and make better choices.

In today's vocabulary, we refer to this as *psychological safety*, a basic need essential for everything from meaningful relationships to solving problems. Which raises a question: If psychological safety is fundamental to human aspiration, how do we make it actionable? This is the question *Safe to Great* seeks to address.

Skip Bowman and I first met as co-facilitators in a leadership development program. What struck me was Skip's intense curiosity, how he listened, prodded, and experimented, learning as much along the way as the participants learned from him. That learning, acquired through years of experience as well as Skip's own research, has been distilled into this valuable leadership guide. Building on the premise that a leader's most important role is to create psychologically safe spaces, this book clarifies the mindsets, skills, and behaviors necessary to achieve that goal.

And yet these "bright side" behaviors are only part of the story. In fact, we've all developed self-protective mechanisms—those autocratic, snarky, or pleasing parts of ourselves that emerge when we feel threatened. It is this understanding of our "dark side" that distinguishes *Safe to Great*—a recognition that leaders are humans too, and that default wiring can erode relationships and sabotage the best-laid plans.

Most of us enter leadership because a person, an idea, a hope, or a challenge has pulled us into the journey—because a nascent sense of purpose tugs at the heart and can't be ignored. Unfortunately, in our rush to meet the next goal or get the next promotion or just survive the next day, we often forget that purpose.

Safe to Great encourages us to recapture those forgotten dreams. Placing the discussion in the context of the great challenges of our times, it asserts that leaders have the power to create safe spaces or demolish them. It dares us to explore our shadows and aspire to our better selves. From here, informed by purpose and liberated from ego, we can focus on outcomes, knowing that great results are achieved only through the collective efforts of people who feel free to dream courageously, speak candidly, and act with commitment in service of better organizations and a better world.

MARTHA FREYMANN MISER, PhD
Founder & President, Aduro Consulting, LLC
Jaffrey, New Hampshire, USA

Introduction

One can choose to go back toward safety or forward toward growth. Growth must be chosen again and again; fear must be overcome again and again.

ABRAHAM MASLOW, *The Psychology of Science*

Surface trouble

Over thirty years ago, I was a diving instructor, accompanying visitors to the Great Barrier Reef in Australia. Much of my approach to my work today as an organizational psychologist, facilitator, and business consultant can be traced back to what I learned then about the importance of psychological safety and its relevance to great leadership. One particular experience with an American in his late twenties, whom I'll call Craig,* taught me a valuable lesson about how to lead amid uncertainty.

* Some names and other identifying details have been changed in this book to protect the people and organizations whose stories were not widely circulated in the media and are not public knowledge.

In October 1990, my colleague Brian and I were responsible for a multinational group of ten divers, most of whom were novices. We were aboard the yacht *Sonja* at Black Reef, about forty nautical miles from the Queensland coast. Early in the morning, I rolled backward into the water from the tinny (aluminum dinghy) with Craig, who was the most experienced diver on the charter.

For thirty minutes we drifted along the coral face, listening to the sounds of mollusks on the reef and the distant song of humpback whales. We were in about a hundred meters of water, twenty-five meters below the ocean surface, and moving quite rapidly in a strong ebbing tide. Everything seemed to be going well.

As we headed back up, we paused for a compression stop at a depth of about eight meters, burning off nitrogen as a safety measure because we'd spent so long in deeper water. I turned around to check on Craig. Gave him the ok hand sign. But he didn't return the gesture. Instead, he pointed. I turned my head and found myself face-to-face with a three-meter-long tiger shark. I knew that I needed to stay calm and not try to swim away. The shark swam past, displaying a characteristic big-toothed grin. For a split second I forgot about Craig. When I turned to check on him, he was gone. I later realized that he'd panicked and raced for the surface. I ascended steadily, keeping the shark in view as it swam away.

When I reached Craig, he had his mask off and was gasping for air. The water was choppy, the result of a stiffening morning breeze, and the low sun glared off its surface. Brian was waiting for us about five hundred meters away in the tinny, but he was looking in the opposite direction, unaware that we had drifted so far. In any case, the water was so choppy, he wouldn't have been able to follow our bubbles to determine where we were.

Craig and I were drifting fast and needed to get to the reef so we could stand up and make it easy for Brian to see us—otherwise we'd end up in the larger basin on the other side of the reef. Craig, though, was still in a state of panic, constantly looking down for the shark. I needed him to calm down so that we could swim across the powerful current. I knew I wouldn't be able to drag him.

The first step was to get Craig to put his mask back on and breathe through his snorkel. The waves were making it hard to talk, and even harder to establish eye contact. Nevertheless, I managed to create a connection, making Craig feel safe enough to follow my instructions and focus on our common purpose, which was getting to the reef without further incident.

What Craig and I went through that October day taught me how vital emotional connection is to psychological safety. Without psychological safety, great leadership is impossible, especially when we feel threatened.

The four new ages

Humanity is facing two threats that are reshaping work and what it is to be human: climate change and AI. Both have the potential to eclipse the economic, social, and technological progress we've made, but they also provide the conditions for a regeneration of our planet and our societies, a "wonderful recovery," as David Attenborough said in his rallying speech to the delegates at COP26 in Cairo in 2021. Understanding these threats and the emerging four new ages they are catalyzing is crucial to understanding the new psychology of leadership I present in this book. These four ages will have an overwhelming impact on both work and the psychological well-being of employees. They're not only challenging us to learn and change but also necessitating major shifts in how we think, behave, and collaborate. Solving the challenges they present requires more than technological innovation. It also requires new ways of relating to the world. If we're to thrive rather than just survive, we'll need a new mindset.

THE GREEN AGE

Unlike Chicxulub, the asteroid that knocked off the dinosaurs, climate change is a human-made threat to our existence that's been creeping up on us for decades. Its impacts aren't immediate, so it's difficult for most people to grasp the full extent of the problem. We have no emotional response for slow-moving threats like sea-level rises—or weight gain. When we aren't aware of things changing and we like things how they are, we struggle to mobilize ourselves and others to take action. We're better at dealing with sharks.

There are exceptions to this rule, though. In 1962, Rachel Carson published *Silent Spring*, in which she warned about the harmful effects of pesticides on the environment, wildlife, and human health. Her dystopian vision of a world without the sounds of insects and birds sparked the environmental movement that ultimately saw the pesticide DDT banned in the USA in 1972. Other landmark agreements followed—for example, bans on lead in gasoline, ozone-destroying gases in refrigerants, and whale-hunting. These changes happened because we grew our mindset. We became aware of a problem and its consequences (we saw); accepted our responsibility for the problem (we cared); mobilized to resolve the problem through activism (we challenged); and united globally and embedded solutions for political change (we collaborated). Luckily these movements weren't dismissed as woke.

The Intergovernmental Panel on Climate Change (IPCC) wants us to limit global warming to a maximum of 2 degrees, but preferably 1.5 degrees. To do this, we need to mobilize the kind of human ingenuity and collaborative effort found most often in times of great hardship (e.g., the COVID-19 pandemic) and more rarely in times of great prosperity (e.g., the Apollo program). We need to become climate warriors. If we don't, the damage wreaked by extreme weather events will threaten our lives in unimaginable ways.

I refer to the transformation of economic activity and society that's required to tackle climate change as the Green Age—an optimistic title, yes, but I believe the optimism is warranted. There are real opportunities to create something great, and we can already see signs of change. New generations of employees are energized by working to save the planet. Investors are demanding companies set and deliver on increasingly ambitious environmental and social goals. Governments are funding innovation and large infrastructure projects to kickstart the transformation, partly to drive new job growth and partly to build more energy independence. And there's proof that our global efforts are paying off. The ozone layer will be repaired by 2060. Watching whales rather than spearing them generated $2 billion in 2009. The last drop of leaded fuel was pumped in Algeria in July 2021.

THE GLOBOTIC AGE

AI isn't a direct threat to our existence unless you're obsessed with movies like *Terminator*. The real threat stems from its consequences for white-collar workers in the US and European service sectors. In his provocative book *The Globotics*

Upheaval, Richard Baldwin outlines how the AI-powered, third Great Transformation of work will seem "monstrously unfair," even by the standards of the two previous great transformations: the industrial revolution (1750-) and the services revolution (1970-). AI and the new wave of globalization will see the loss of well-paid jobs outstrip the creation of new, potentially better-paid jobs. McKinsey estimates that between 2016 and 2030, approximately 400 million workers–15% of the global workforce–could be displaced, maybe many more, depending on how quickly smart machines are deployed. The ability of people to retrain fast enough for the new jobs that do emerge will depend greatly on how governments and the corporate world respond to the challenge. Furthermore, the jobs will be distributed more globally than previously. AI will enable people in emerging economies to leapfrog many decades of technological development in the West. According to Baldwin, this will drive a new and far more disruptive wave of stay-at-home globalization.

Edward Hess and Katherine Ludwig argue in their optimistic book *Humility is the New Smart* that to win the race against the machines, we must replace our industrial-era "old smart" skills, based on knowledge retention, with "new smart" skills like quieting the ego, managing self, reflective listening, and recognizing otherness. New smart is measured "not by quantity–how much you know–but by the quality of your thinking, learning, and emotionally engaging with others." To compete, we must focus on human-human collaboration, developing our ability to collaborate creatively and critically with each other. That is, we must become better team players rather than going solo to try to outsmart robots.

We'll also need to rapidly develop human-robot collaboration, what I like to call corobotics. Working with AI will change how and what we learn. When AI can deliver customized knowledge in seconds based on our complex and even misspelled questions, why should I take a lecture, listen to a podcast, or participate in online learning?

Ready or not, like it or not, we've entered the Globotic Age, a space and time where humans will need to collaborate 24/7 with robots and people from around the world. I've already become more globotic. My editor, Lesley, lives and works in British Columbia. While I sleep in Copenhagen, she edits my manuscript. While I write, ChatGPT answers my research questions. Sometimes ChatGPT gets things wrong, so we have that in common with each other.

THE CARING AGE

Leading authors writing about the threats of climate change and AI agree that if we want to avoid some very nasty outcomes, we need to care a lot more about each other and the planet. In *Future on Fire: Capitalism and the Politics of Climate Change*, the labor studies and sociology professor David Camfield argues that we need a "just transition" that delivers on the IPCC goals and reduces social injustice. Unchecked capitalism and existing social structures won't deliver on either of these goals, he says. Furthermore, Baldwin writes that "the new phases of globalization and robotics need to be seen by most people as fair, equitable, and inclusive." He believes that we must create policies that help people adapt, make the changes politically acceptable (and maybe more gradual), and share the economic pain by addressing income inequality, lack of access to learning, and poverty. We need *good growth* rather than profit-based growth.

At a more literal level, the imbalance between the number of young and old people and the rising level of mental illness across all age groups will necessitate more careworkers. The UN estimates that the global population of people over sixty-five will double from 703 million in 2019 to 1.5 billion in 2050. The National Institutes of Health estimates that one in five American adults suffers from mental illness during any given year. Furthermore, the American Psychological Association reports that the new generation of workers shows higher levels of mental illness due partly to "the rise of electronic communication and digital media and declines in sleep duration" since the mid-2000s. No wonder the health-care industry is the USA's largest employer.

However, there are signs that we've entered the Caring Age—yes, I know, another optimistic title. The evolution of environment, social, and governance (ESG) targets and reporting is a clear example of how many investors are demanding a shift from profit-only to a broader and fairer set of objectives. Governments in New Zealand and Finland are exploring how to redefine prosperity to replace GDP as the sole measure of progress. Companies, too, are beginning to realize that they need to show a different level of care about employees, at least in terms of support for learning and change. Amazon has implemented the Upskilling 2025 program, investing $700 million for employees to acquire new skills in or outside of the company. JPMorgan Chase has committed $350 million over five years to transition employees to new roles as automation and AI change their work. AT&T has a Future Ready program for all employees and IBM has a New Collar initiative to train blue-collar workers for high-tech roles.

THE DIGITAL ENLIGHTENMENT AGE

According to Douglas Rushkoff, media theorist, professor, and author of *Team Human*, in the first few decades since

Internet access became more widely available and social media became popular, we've seen authoritarian, criminal, and commercial forces exploit these technologies and our use of them. We're in the "dark age of social media," according to the computer scientist Diego Queirós. The Internet was supposed to be the great democratizer. Now it seems like one of the most insidious threats to our freedom. The platforms that enable us to share information and photos with friends and family, and organize for positive political change, have been weaponized against us by autocrats, monopolists, terrorist groups, and rich playboys who want to rewrite democratic, economic, and social rules to promote their less democratic and unfair visions of the world.

Rushkoff argues that humans need to reassert their humanity in the face of technological advancement and the efficiency of algorithmic thinking: "We must learn to see the technologically accelerated social, political, and economic chaos ahead of us as an invitation for more willful participation. It's not a time to condemn the human activity that's brought us to this point, but to infuse this activity with more human and humane priorities."

Fortunately, we've begun to fight back with policy, policing, and new digital practices. Digital privacy legislation, transparency, and accountability for tech companies as news providers; fact-checking technology; and digital literacy training for children are all early signs of the Digital Enlightenment. But to keep our freedom and prevent machine-made catastrophes, we'll need "cyber" critical thinking. At home, this can protect and liberate us from fake news, fake choices, and fake politics. At work, it can lead to new ethical standards and checks to ensure that our ability to track, film, and otherwise control employees doesn't create a hellish psychological gulag.

The four ages offer hope. However, I'm not blind to the fact that many people are anxious and fearful about the current and future changes. As Baldwin notes about the past transformations, "the iron law of globalization and automation is that progress means change, and change means pain." We must make it easier for people to adjust and grow. As a species, we must create safety if we're to realize our full potential.

This is the right backdrop against which we can learn to understand how leadership must evolve in the coming years. The first step is creating psychological safety.

Psychological safety

People who feel safe share more information, which leads to better learning, quality, and innovation.

In a 2017 *Harvard Business Review (HBR)* article, the psychologist and Stanford University instructor Laura Delizonna looks at a two-year study conducted by Google and research by the social psychologist Barbara Fredrickson at the University of North Carolina into the factors driving high performance in software development teams. Psychological safety is the common denominator among the teams studied. Failure and all its consequences are possible, but learning is inevitable whatever the outcome. Among these teams, "positive emotions like trust, curiosity, confidence, and inspiration broaden the mind and help us build psychological, social, and physical resources. We become more open-minded, resilient, motivated, and persistent when we feel safe. Humor increases, as does solution-finding and divergent thinking—the cognitive process underlying creativity."

This connection between positive relationships and innovation was originally discovered by the Harvard professor and leadership expert Amy Edmondson. In her book *The Fearless*

Organization, she shares how she discovered the significance of psychological safety while researching surgical teams in the late 1990s. Paradoxically, surgical teams that reported the most errors were also the teams that learned and innovated the most. Psychological safety in teams encouraged people to speak up, and this created learning and innovation. It also improved quality. For Edmondson, the biggest barrier to learning is fear. Fear keeps our mouths tightly shut, even when we know that speaking up could make for a better workplace or even save lives. This is termed the "conspiracy of silence" in the book *Crucial Conversations: Tools for Talking When Stakes Are High* by Kerry Patterson, Joseph Grenny, Ron McMillan, and Al Switzler.

These findings are the foundation for the Safe2Great model that I elaborate on below. But there's more to the idea of psychological safety.

A second perspective on psychological safety considers how the threats of the four ages and current organizational practices combine to create poor conditions for mental health in the workplace. Manfred Kets de Vries, professor of leadership development and organizational change at INSEAD, argues that we're experiencing a collective slide into fear and anxiety that's been provoked substantially by the isolation we experienced during COVID-19 lockdowns, social media addiction, and corporate work practices. Our resulting lack of real, as opposed to virtual, connection to others has made us vulnerable to conspiracies and the rhetoric of demagogues.

In this sense, psychological safety becomes more than an idea to promote learning and innovation. It can also help us reduce stress, burnout, and anxiety in society as a whole.

A third perspective is based on my research, which shows that many leaders create inadequate psychological safety through controlling leadership. Consequently, employees are becoming poorer team players. Controlling leaders focus almost exclusively on individual goals and development plans and require people to follow the script rather than use their wits. In this way, they block the development of mentally healthy teams and employees. Cynical thinking is more common in our organizations than optimism, and, according to the author and researcher Christine Porath, incivility and toxicity are increasing. We're becoming less kind and less forgiving.

A fourth perspective on psychological safety is more sinister. A lack of psychological safety and a conspiracy of silence are almost always at the heart of corporate scandals (e.g., Enron, Wells Fargo, Danske Bank, Boeing, and Volkswagen's "Dieselgate"). In *Faster, Higher, Farther: The Volkswagen Scandal*, the *New York Times* journalist Jack Ewing argues that Volkswagen's relentless pursuit of growth and profitability, coupled with a culture of secrecy and fear, created an environment in which engineers and managers felt pressured to cheat on emissions tests to meet aggressive sales targets and performance goals. In these cases, a lack of psychological safety was arguably intentional.

These scandals can seem like outliers in our highly regulated, audited, and transparent business world. However, as I discuss in detail below, a culture of fear is more common and also more tempting to create than you might think.

Edmondson writes: "I have defined psychological safety as the belief that the work environment is safe for interpersonal risk taking. The concept refers to the experience of feeling able to speak up with relevant ideas, questions, or concerns. Psychological safety is present when colleagues trust and respect each other and feel able—even obligated—to be candid." Her definition of psychological safety resonates deeply with me in my work. It promotes a robust, dynamic, and candid relationship between leaders and employees. It's not about comfort, but rather the discomfort of speaking the truth even when it challenges egos, disrupts the conspiracy of silence, and blows whistles. A new psychology of leadership needs to make people safe.

However, it won't be enough to feel safe at work. A new psychology of leadership must address the lack of existential safety in our work and personal lives, and in society in general. If we fear we'll lose our jobs to AI, we won't do our best work. We need a compassionate form of leadership that reconnects people to each other and the physical world, invites them to contribute and realize their dreams, and nurtures an increasingly diverse workforce. Companies can't—and shouldn't—protect people from the changes that lie ahead, but they can moderate the brutality of the journey for employees, customers, and citizens.

Psychological safety offers hope for making workplaces more inclusive, open, and effective. However, it doesn't solve all the challenges of the four ages, and it can't even exist unless we tackle workplace burnout and stress.

Workplace burnout

Work is more demanding, mentally and socially, than ever. In fact, it's burning people out at an unprecedented rate.

In 2019, the WHO defined "burnout" as a significant occupational disease "resulting from chronic workplace stress that has not been successfully managed...characterized by... feelings of energy depletion or exhaustion; increased mental distance from one's job, or feelings of negativism or cynicism related to one's job; and reduced professional efficacy." It's especially common among people who work in the care-based industries. Jobs that are complex, people-related, and emotional are some of the hardest to survive, and they comprise a significant proportion of the work that will exist in the future. But more about that later.

Two important drivers of workplace burnout are collaboration and cognitive overload. In their 2016 article "Collaborative Overload," Rob Cross, Reb Rebele, and Adam Grant claim that "collaborative activities have ballooned by 50% or more" between 1996 and 2016. They argue that the rise of collaborative technologies and the trend toward flatter, more team-based organizational structures have led to a situation in which many workers are overwhelmed by demands for their time and expertise. They suggest that technology is partly to blame for this problem. Email, social media, instant messaging, and videoconferencing have all made it easier than ever to connect with colleagues at any time of day or night, but they've also inflated expectations about how accessible we should be.

Cognitive overload is the stress we feel when we have too much information and too much complexity. Our world is increasingly volatile, uncertain, complex, ambiguous, and hyper-connected (VUCAH). In addition, we must deal with an extraordinary amount of information in our jobs. It's increasingly difficult to separate symptoms from causes, facts from fakes, and social media from what I see in my mirror every morning. It's harder to make decisions, especially collective ones. In "Designing Organizations for an Information-Rich World," Nobel Prize–winning economist and social scientist Herbert Simon wrote, "In an information-rich world, the wealth of information means a dearth of something else: a scarcity of whatever it is that information consumes. What information consumes is . . . the attention of its recipients.

Hence, a wealth of information creates a poverty of attention..." In other words, our minds become frazzled by too much information, too much multitasking, and too many distractions. (Simon wrote those words in 1971. I can't imagine how he'd express it now.)

The most common symptoms of workplace overload are exhaustion or fatigue, impatience and intolerance for others' mistakes, loss of focus and attention to detail, difficulty making decisions, irritability and restlessness, and anxiety and depression. We can see the impact of overload in data measuring employee well-being, stress, and burnout and in the recent focus on quiet quitting (people who are psychologically withdrawn from their work, doing as little as possible to get by).

According to Steven Sloman and Philip Fernbach, not only is work fundamentally collaborative, so too is intelligence. In their 2015 book, *The Knowledge Illusion: Why We Never Think Alone,* they write: "Our intelligence resides not in individual brains but in the collective mind. To function, individuals rely not only on knowledge stored within our skulls but also on knowledge stored elsewhere: in our bodies, in the environment, and especially in other people. When you put it all together, human thought is incredibly impressive. But it is a product of a community, not of any individual alone." They argue that "social sensitivity" is one of the best predictors of a high team intelligence. Unfortunately, this also implies that when collaboration fails, we not only get stressed but we also get a lot less intelligent.

I'm obsessed with collaboration, because it really is the best way to solve big problems and to share the workload more fairly and sustainably. A new psychology of leadership must be based on caring and effective relationships. It must make us better team players. However, what I see today are organizational cultures and leadership practices built almost exclusively around one-to-one relationships. Hyper-individualized approaches to leadership and learning, in addition to virtual teams, distance work, selective engagement, and micro-targeting, encourage people to withdraw psychologically, isolate physically, and become alienated. This trend was exacerbated by responses to the COVID-19 pandemic—it wasn't caused by it, contrary to what many people believe. Hyper-individualization promises jobs that suit individual employees' needs and skills, but it also creates lonely and disconnected people who don't know who or how to ask for help, can't discuss innovative ideas, and can't make decisions.

Workplace overload can be experienced at the individual, team, and organizational level. Demands on the system outstrip the available capabilities and resources. We begin to operate in a "red zone." Operating for too long in the red zone leads to a breakdown or decay of the system. We become less productive and burn out. Unless, that is, we consider how to reorganize or transform our way of operating. The solution I propose is not more individual responsibility but rather a more collaborative and growing mindset.

Mindset

What is mindset?

In 2006, Carol Dweck published *Mindset: The New Psychology of Success*, in which she introduced the concept of "growth" and "fixed" mindsets. Her ideas took a while to become popular, but today they're almost ubiquitous in leadership workshops. Mindset is the new language of leadership. Understanding and mastering it can help you to become a great leader, develop safer and more productive teams, and create more adaptive, greener, and fairer organizations.

Mindset isn't a skill, competency, or attitude. Nor is it synonymous with personality. Definitions vary, but I see it as similar to "consciousness," a self-aware, self-regulating, and semi-autonomous form of mental activity that weaves feelings, senses, thoughts, and actions into patterns of relating to the world.

A simple analogy will help me explain. Imagine you're sitting in your car right now, on the way to work, a client meeting, or Disneyland with the kids. Your mindset is how you're currently driving in response to what's going on inside you, inside the car, and in the traffic around you. Sometimes we drive carefully and consciously; when it's raining, for example. Sometimes we drive recklessly and wildly, such as when we're in a hurry. Sometimes, we drive distractedly while texting a friend—unconsciously and dangerously. How you drive depends on the kind of journey you're on. Journeys vary in terms of length, difficulty, terrain, planning, familiarity, and purpose. If work was like a regular commute, then it may be okay to drive the same way every day. But work isn't like a commute. From one meeting to the next, you often must adapt to completely different kinds of traffic conditions, journeys, and most importantly different driving styles.

Personality tests, IQ assessments, and psychological profiles can tell us something about the qualities, characteristics, and capabilities of you and your car. Mindset tells us how you respond to the road and traffic and get to your destination safely and quickly. Dweck is right to say that some people work at becoming safer, better, and more versatile drivers. They grow. Others get stuck or fixed, thinking they already know how to drive anywhere better than anyone else.

Mindset, like the way we drive our real car, allows us to make the most of what we have and sometimes to surpass our current capabilities and preferences. It can also make even getting out of the garage a seemingly insurmountable challenge.

To explore some of the different perspectives of mindset, let me take the example of humility, which Jim Collins singles out as one of the key attributes of great leaders in *Good to Great*, the title of which has inspired this book and the concept of Safe to Great. Achieving humility is a little more complicated than you might think. It involves managing and integrating elements of your internal world like emotions and thoughts and linking them to the outer world via empathy and cooperative action. Most people don't spend much time reflecting on humility or how they drive, which is a pity.

From an emotional perspective, humility involves being able to regulate biological drives and emotions. Sometimes this means taming negative emotions or exuberance. Sometimes it's about resetting and recovering from the anger and disappointment of failure. Sometimes, it's knowing how to remain calm and receptive as people criticize your best work.

Cognitively, humility involves recognizing and accepting your limitations, being open to feedback and learning, and being curious. The John Templeton Foundation defines intellectual humility as the ability to "overcome responses to evidence that are self-centered or that outstrip the strength of that evidence. This mindset encourages us to seek out and evaluate ideas and information in such a way that we are less influenced by our own motives and more oriented toward discovery of the truth."

Behaviorally, humility involves acting in ways that demonstrate respect for others, such as asking deep questions, responding openly to feedback, showing support for others' ideas, suspending judgment, and avoiding arrogance.

From a social perspective, humility requires that our humble behaviors are interpreted as authentic. Done wrong or insincerely, humility can easily be interpreted as cockiness, disingenuity, or faintheartedness.

The last ingredient is the situation. Maybe humility is the wrong thing to display in terms of creating a great outcome? Humility is an effective way of driving in some situations, but it may not suit when others are driving aggressively or too cautiously or giving you the bird. We also need to imagine showing humility when it's the last thing our damaged pride wants to do. Humility in these situations requires defying our natural responses to adversity and setbacks, like driving slowly when we're in a hurry to prevent an accident or a traffic jam.

I noted above that mindset isn't synonymous with personality. That's because it evolves via experiences, and we can change it via reflection. Our mindset gets "upgraded," or grows, particularly during childhood and early adulthood. An upgrade can go unnoticed, but you may recall moments when you became aware of your ability to manage more, do more, see more. Events like going to university, getting your first job, learning a new language, being promoted to your first leadership role, or becoming a parent are all candidates for this type of upgrade. In these cases, you didn't just learn something new, you became someone new. Your personality didn't change, but you learned to drive better, getting more out of the car, road, and journey.

Sometimes upgrades are born out of adversity, necessity, or a calamity like when we lose our job, one of our parents dies, or our business goes bankrupt. Hopefully these negative experiences lead to positive learning in the form of growth. We become better drivers from smaller accidents. But accidents, especially big ones, can also lead us to un-grow, to regress into more protective and defensive mindsets.

Other upgrades are born out of an epiphany. We're talking Archimedes in the bathtub, or me realizing that I wanted to be a psychologist rather than an accountant. Suddenly the way we've been understanding ourselves and the world up until that moment seems just plain wrong. We embark on a new journey with a mindset that has grown.

For many people, their mindset helps them make sense of the world and their role in it in ways that support positive self-esteem and confidence. For others, it can make them feel like an impostor, weak, or like a victim or, conversely, superior, entitled, and above the law. In this way, mindset is part fact but mostly story. The more it's based on fact the better it is for our health and for those around us in the traffic.

Your mindset is partly of your own making, partly shaped by how important people in your life relate to the world, and partly influenced by the mindset of people you meet on the way into the office. It's both stable and situational. You might feel positive when you arrive at the office, but you may not stay that way if the security guard makes your life hard when you discover you forgot your access card. We influence each other's mindset a great deal more than we think. It seeps into us by way of emotions. This is both good and bad. Good, because it suggests that we can nudge people into relating more positively to the world. Bad, because it suggests that negative team experiences and poor relationships are contagious. We're all susceptible to road rage. If we're exposed to lots of negative people, especially our tailgating boss, we're more likely to un-grow. Or resign.

Protective mindsets

I've worked as an organizational psychologist specializing in leadership for twenty-five years. In that time I've seen good, bad, tough-but-fair, destructive, tyrannical, narcissistic, and hopeless leaders. Occasionally, I've seen leaders from the more authoritarian end of the spectrum achieve adequate, even good, results. I'm always struck by how often these controlling leaders have missed opportunities to strengthen the emotional connections that drive excellence and growth.

I often imagine how things might have turned out in critical moments if those leaders had trusted their people, delegated more, and listened more attentively; taken more risks or communicated a bolder vision; or built confidence and hope. What could have been if they'd played for great. Instead, when doubt prevailed and ego was threatened, I've seen too many leaders choose to protect themselves. They play it safe by instructing everyone to maintain the status quo, relying on their own ideas and making all the decisions, and checking everyone else's work and demanding more and better. While they experienced a sense of personal safety or the thrill of being in charge, the people around them experienced controlling and toxic leadership. Trust, engagement, and openness declined, while blame, stress, and turnover increased.

My research confirms that controlling leadership is less effective than most people think. Paradoxically, controlling leaders usually have offices adorned with certificates proclaiming positive organizational values like empowerment, shelves with books about humility, and personal development goals that include developing growth-minded behaviors like listening, delegating, and encouraging. And yet they continue to control rather than trust, especially when they face challenge, change, or uncertainty.

How do we explain the gap between what these leaders know they should do and what they actually do? The answer is found in two words: protective mindsets.

There are three types of protective mindsets: controlling, complying, and cynical. Leaders operate with a protective mindset because they experience strong payoffs for doing so. Basically, some leaders get a kick out of bossing people around (controlling), feel loved by keeping everyone happy (complying), or relish their unique intellect by insulting others sarcastically (cynical).

Protective mindsets make you feel safe and others feel unsafe. For example, acting tough gives many leaders a feeling of control and power, and wins them admiration from like-minded bosses, board members, and the stock market. It can lead to career success—but it's not very effective, because it increases cognitive and collaborative overload in others and reduces psychological safety.

Protective mindsets are coping rather than creative strategies. We're operating with a protective mindset when we retreat from complex challenges and uncertainty and focus our energy on internal fears or threats. Controlling leaders are more worried about looking like being in control than about solving problems. If they don't know how to solve a real problem, they focus their energy on showing that they're in charge, even though the problem stays unsolved. Complying leaders are more worried about having good relationships than solving problems, so when they're in doubt about what to do, they're nice to everyone. Cynical leaders are more worried about looking smart than solving problems, so they criticize everyone else and undermine every new idea. I explore protective mindsets in more detail in Part II.

From safe to great

What would the world look like if leaders in industry chose to make people safe?

In October 1987, when Paul O'Neill spoke to the world about the power of worker safety to drive a turnaround in the fortunes of Alcoa, where he had just taken on the role of president, he did so knowing he needed a transformational agenda that spoke to the employees' needs and ambitions. Under O'Neill's tenure, Alcoa implemented a comprehensive change program that made safety central to its culture, turning the company around and making it a leader in safety, productivity, and employee engagement.

I learned of Alcoa's transformation in Charles Duhigg's book, *The Power of Habit*. Duhigg, who's interested in how we make changes happen, uses the Alcoa story to highlight the importance of a "keystone habit," the one thing that unites leaders, employees, and other stakeholders in a positive cycle of growth and change. At Alcoa, O'Neill's keystone habit was demanding that leaders at all levels of the organization respond to safety issues and injuries immediately. They literally had to report to O'Neill about safety issues and solutions within twenty-four hours. This habit encouraged employees to report all injuries, no matter how minor, and managers used the information to identify and eliminate sources of danger. Alcoa also launched a comprehensive injury management program to give employees the medical treatment and support they needed after an injury.

Alcoa's efforts paid off. The injury rate fell dramatically, and the company's productivity and profitability improved as a result. The culture of safety also led to increased employee morale and engagement. Workers felt that the company valued their well-being, and many were proud to work for an organization that prioritized safety.

The Alcoa story demonstrates how caring about employees can transform effort, collaboration, and well-being. It's just the recipe we need for leaders and organizations in the four ages. Many things have changed since the 1990s, but I believe we can learn much from the story about great leadership and about rapid change.

The research

In 2015, I decided to create a new concept that combined the ideas of psychological safety and growth mindset in a single model about leadership and organizational culture. I started off by investigating the working styles of great leaders who work effectively in collaborative, creative, and constructive spaces—that is, people who aren't only personally successful but also help create great teams and great organizations. What are their patterns of relating to the world in terms of thinking, feeling, and acting?

Having spent fifteen years working with models that measured behavioral and cultural patterns, I knew there was a lot of good research to build on about motivation, innovation, purpose, emotional intelligence, learning, and collaboration. I wanted to integrate existing thinking with new ideas and recast them in terms of emerging challenges like climate change, smart machines, and poor mental health.

First, I created six growth leadership principles that drew on both new research and important established high-performance principles. Second, I defined ten protective principles by reviewing work by experts including John Kotter, Daniel Goleman, and Lynda Gratton on dysfunctional leadership behaviors and organizational cultures.

One of the most common ways to categorize behaviors is along the task vs. people focus continuum. I theorized that growth would be most likely to occur when people created the optimal balance of challenge (task focus) and encouragement (people focus) in their relationships.

Three of the growth principles are task-focused and depend on intrinsic motivators such as purpose, self-determination, excellence, and learning: Transform, Aim High, and Explore. The other three are people-focused and build on prosocial motivators such as positive energy, recognition, fairness, and connection: Go High, Lift Others Up, and Team Up. I explain these in detail in Part I.

The next step was to turn these ideas into a set of measurement tools that could map the connection between mindset and other important outcomes like effectiveness, commitment, and psychological safety. My team and I created four tools: the Growth Mindset Leadership 360, Great Teams assessment, Change Champion tool, and Culture for Growth survey. We compare the results produced by these tools against our global benchmarks to enable us to compare leaders, teams, and organizations in terms of the six growth principles and three protective mindsets. With these tools, we can map not only how growth-minded you really are, but also the extent to which you operate with protective mindsets.

Eight years later, and with thousands of leaders and global companies across the world assessed, I can confirm that leaders who practice the six growth principles and release themselves from their protective alternatives create significantly more effective teams, build stronger commitment, and develop a strong sense of psychological safety.

Growth mindset

Believing in growth is one thing; thinking, feeling, and acting in alignment with this belief is another.

Dweck defines growth mindset as "the belief that your basic qualities are things you can cultivate through your efforts, your strategies, and help from others. Although people may differ in every which way—in their initial talents and aptitudes, interests, or temperaments—everyone can change and grow through application and experience." In other words, growth-minded leaders get a kick out of personal learning and change, not just making others learn and change—that's what a leader with a protective mindset loves.

Earlier, I defined mindset as a self-aware, self-regulating, and semi-autonomous form of mental activity that weaves feelings, senses, thoughts, and actions into patterns of relating to the world—and how you drive your car. It follows that people with a growth mindset have developed the ability to unpick old patterns and weave new ones more regularly and more confidently in response to failure, adversity, and opportunity. They adapt their way of driving to road and traffic conditions and the journey they're on. These new patterns allow them to embrace more complexity and mobilize more cognitive, emotional, and physical resources. They grow rather than un-grow. Growth-minded people show commitment to a vision, effective planning, curiosity, collaboration, encouragement, and grit in the face of adversity.

In my definition of growth mindset, I've added a new component to Dweck's original definition that reflects the intrinsically social nature of our lives and work. If collaboration and care really are the most important skills in the four ages, we need to include how people with a growth mindset, great leaders for instance, connect with and mobilize the efforts and talents of others. At work, we aren't only trying to drive to our destination, but also trying to help others get to their destination safely and quickly. Sometimes we're on the same journey; sometimes we meet at a traffic circle or an uncontrolled intersection, going in completely different directions. These are the situations my theory of growth mindset is designed to help us with.

People with a growth mindset weave increasingly prosocial and proactive patterns of thinking that encourage and mobilize the cognitive, emotional, and physical resources of the people around them and help them grow.

They help others to drive better as they improve the effectiveness of their own driving.

If the role of leaders is to create more leaders, not followers, the role of growth-minded leaders is to create more people with a growth mindset, not people with a protective mindset. Growth-minded people display energy and positivity, help others to take risks and learn, include people who are different, and collaborate in the face of adversity.

In *Multipliers*, her study of leadership impact on organizational performance, Liz Wiseman demonstrates how the most effective leaders amplify the capabilities of their colleagues. They show what's possible, encouraging others to share their ideas, extend themselves, and throw off the inhibitions that restrain them. To explain this phenomenon, I often refer to the recent success of Tom Brady at the Tampa Bay Buccaneers American football franchise.

Prior to signing for the Buccaneers in 2020, Tom Brady was regarded by many as the greatest quarterback of all time, having enjoyed huge success with the New England Patriots, a team with which he won six Super Bowl titles between 2001 and 2018. By contrast, the Buccaneers, one-time winners of the Super Bowl in 2002, were on a run of thirteen consecutive years without reaching the end-of-season playoffs. On joining the Buccaneers, Brady didn't rest on his laurels. He brought to the pre-season training camp a desire to keep learning and improving, mental toughness harnessed with a relentless desire to win, and the ability to keep performing to a high standard under pressure.

Through his work ethic and his commitment to and expectations of others, Brady had just such a multiplying effect on his teammates and coaches, ultimately unlocking their relational potential.

Over the course of the 2020-21 season, the team progressed from being perennial also-rans to Super Bowl champions, and forty-three-year-old Brady was rated MVP in the final for the fifth time.

Brady's story is a simple example of what I mean by thinking about growth mindset as more than a theory about learning. It's a theory about how to create great teams and organizations. It's also the inspiration for my elevator pitch definition of growth mindset:

> Growth mindset is our ability to bring out the best in ourselves (personal potential) and the best in others (relational potential).

This definition provides a framework for the first trajectory of human development in the four ages—how to make the most of human-human collaboration and realize relational potential. The second trajectory of human development is toward a philosophy of growth that farms the physical resources of the Earth rather than mines them, that nurtures human resources rather than exploits them. I call this *good growth.*

The third trajectory of human development is toward corobotics. How do we harness the power of AI and smart machines to make life and work more meaningful and healthier for humans rather than use them as an instrument exclusively for profit?

To grow as a person is to become capable of more when working with others and with robots (an awkward but entirely relevant goal). To grow as an organization is to cultivate and combine resources more thoughtfully and effectively, and to connect with other organizations to create ecosystems of sustainable growth. To grow as a community is to embrace new ways of living and new people in an inclusive, safe, and prosperous society.

To shift into a growth mindset, as I discovered on the Great Barrier Reef with Craig, we must learn how to keep ourselves safe and make others feel safe in tough situations. Not the kind of safety that the "weak" pursue and the "tough" peddle, but an active, collaborative, and innovative safety. This is the "secure base" George Kohlrieser writes about in *Care to Dare.* We reach for something better, knowing that someone has our back if we struggle or meet resistance.

About this book

When I started writing this book, I wasn't sure how leadership had changed or was changing. It's so easy to fall into the trap of considering leadership timeless, that what Aristotle, Lao Tzu, and Shakespeare wrote about leadership applies equally today. Now I realize that leadership isn't changing, and nor was I, or at least not quickly enough. The truth is that the world and the role we as humans play in it are changing dramatically. The message of Safe to Great becomes more relevant, at least in my head, with every page I turn when I'm reading about the future of work. Creating safe relationships, safe workplaces, safe societies, and a safe world really is the foundation for realizing something great.

I wrote this book because I want to use my experience and knowledge of leadership development to change the world. I have a dream that the Safe2Great model will help us thrive in the four ages. I also dream of a world where plastic products not only have the potential to be recycled and reused but are actually recycled and reused. Where COVID-19, malaria, and other diseases are eradicated. And, call me biased since I have four daughters (and a son), where women participate equally in all aspects of society.

In this book, I consider not only how a growth mindset positively impacts personal learning and effectiveness, but also how it contributes to improving team capabilities like collaboration, innovation, and organizational agility—that is, how does a growth mindset improve how we work together? I also look at growth mindset in the context of great leadership—that is, what does leadership with a growth mindset look like? This I call the bright side of leadership (Part I). Of course, you can't have a bright side without a dark side. So, in Part II I look at protective mindsets. What are they? Why are they so common? What are the consequences of a protective mindset? And how do we create a culture for growth? Finally, I look at how we can integrate the bright and dark sides into an approach for personal and organizational development. How can we help people with a protective mindset shift to a growth mindset?

This is more a book about "why" than "how." I wrote it to explain how psychological safety and growth mindset can create great organizations, the kind that can contribute to the green neighborhoods, cities, and industries of the future. It's not a textbook. It's more of a prompt. I want to nudge you to take an honest look at yourself and your organization and then come up with your own ideas. I want to disrupt how leadership is currently practiced in approximately 70% of organizations around the world. I want to rebalance the uneven playing field and unfairness of organizations due to the prevalence of controlling leaders. Don't look for direct answers to the questions I pose. Treat them as prompts to examine your own mindset.

The Safe2Great model is a practicable set of principles that can be applied to meet the challenges of leading and organizing in the four ages. This model isn't for everyone. It's for leaders who want commitment, sustainability, and social responsibility engrained in everything they do; who want to put people, purpose, and prosperity before profit; and who want to bring more hope and critical thinking to how leaders manage. If you're reading this book, you're probably one of them.

The next chapter

What does great leadership look like? Well, I think it looks like a pod of dolphins.

PART I

The Bright Side

Why is commitment the goal of
growth-minded leaders?

What are great examples of leadership
and organizational culture?

What are the core principles of growth
mindset at work?

How do we combine growth mindset
and psychological safety?

What can leaders do to facilitate
growth mindset?

1

The Commitment Premium

What is commitment and how is it more powerful and sustainable than control?

Departure

As I was about to board a plane recently, I glanced through the window of the jetway and saw a member of the ground crew leaning far into the engine on the aircraft's left wing. I found myself strongly hoping that the individual conducting this inspection had a growth mindset. If they did, I knew they would go beyond a routine tick-box exercise for the safety check. I knew that they'd be able to not only identify old problems but also notice emerging unforeseen ones. Essentially, they'd be a curious, creative human problem-solver, rather than a machine that could work only within the parameters of its existing knowledge.

When working through a safety checklist, a safety inspector requires absolute focus to shut out all distractions. But they also need to be curious, alert, and attentive to anomalies, abnormalities, and the unexpected—to details not captured by a standardized procedure. In a complex work environment where having a growth mindset is the norm, going off-script when necessary is actively encouraged. People feel able to respond and adapt to contextual changes and nuance; to be a proactive problem-solver and interact with others and smart machines to get a second opinion.

An inspector with a growth mindset wouldn't be deferential to hierarchy or process, but would feel enabled to speak up, to question and challenge other ground and flight crew, raising concerns and flagging issues, even delaying the flight if they felt it was necessary.

I realized that my safety and my fellow passengers' safety depended in part on the mindset of this inspector and their colleagues. Without a growth mindset, there's more risk, more room for error and omission. Bracing for impact and trying to put on a life jacket in preparation for a "water landing" is not on my bucket list. Watching this individual at work, though, inspired trust and confidence. I stepped onto the plane, convinced that I'd seen a Dolphin in action. Confident that I wouldn't be wrestling with the life jacket today.

"Dolphin?" I hear you ask. Metaphors are a great way to communicate complex ideas like growth mindset in big organizations. Animals are particularly useful because, like so many other aspects of the natural world, they're familiar and usually inspire us. They can also make us laugh—especially when we see some element of our own behavior in theirs.

The Dolphin

Dolphins are smart, agile, dynamic creatures. They work collaboratively in often dangerous, invariably complex, competitive environments. They play together to reinforce social bonds and communicate constantly—whistling while they work. They're perceived as friendly and approachable. But they're no pushover, no easy touch. They have sharp teeth. When I was growing up, I often visited a pod of dolphins at Monkey Mia in Western Australia, one of the only places in the world where wild dolphins chose to interact with humans. I've loved them from the first time I looked into their deep and intelligent eyes. I also count *Flipper,* a TV series from the 1960s, as one of my favorite American shows.

In the Safe2Great model, Dolphins are leaders who choose growth rather than protection, particularly when facing adversity and challenge. Dolphins have personal strength, but they also build strong, inclusive pods, leveraging relational potential to deliver results that far exceed those of leaders with a protective mindset. And of course, they fight off sharks.

Dolphin-led organizations are trusting and trustworthy. In the face of constant change, they accept the necessity of taking risks, solving problems collectively, and learning from both missteps and successes. Their people hold each other, including themselves, accountable. They have integrity, are candid with one another, and seek to do good for their colleagues, their stakeholders, and the wider community.

Their curiosity, desire to improve, and willingness to listen and learn all have a catalytic effect on their teammates, shaping and fomenting organizational culture. The Dolphin asks questions and encourages new ideas, makes suggestions, and sets goals. They nudge the organization forward rather than remaining stuck in the status quo, in yesterday's knowledge and practices. The Dolphin's constructive approach is founded on care for others, purposeful intent, attention to detail, and a willingness to act.

To borrow the terminology of Liz Wiseman, the Dolphin is a *multiplier*. Their own growth mindset feeds the collective growth mindset, and vice versa. The Dolphin nurtures and serves others, harnessing their knowledge, energy, and enthusiasm for the common good. Compare this with the image of the solitary, heroic leader commanding others and making all the decisions alone. The Dolphin inspires confidence, establishes competence, encourages exploration and experimentation, and brings out the best in others. When their teammates thrive, the Dolphin thrives. When the Dolphin experiences growth, the team experiences growth. When the Dolphin leaps to the challenge, the other members of the pod follow them with a vigorous leap out of the water.

For an example of how Dolphins multiply others' talents, let's look at the English Test Cricket team and the phenomenon of Bazball. It might be a strange choice for readers in the USA, but I love Test cricket. I then explore growth mindset in action at Microsoft.

Bazball

The 2021-22 season was not going well for the England Men's Test Cricket team. By the end of March 2022, they had only won one Test (a five-day-long game) in seventeen Test matches. The time was right for a change of leadership. In mid-April, Rob Key became the new managing director of England Men's Cricket. Shortly after, he appointed Brendon "Baz" McCullum coach and promoted Ben Stokes to captain. These were unlikely choices for coach and captain, but Key wanted to bring something new and unorthodox to the game. The vision the three men implemented for the team was affectionately known as Bazball. It involved creating a stronger connection to the fans, the Barmy Army, fostering a playful team culture so players enjoyed playing more, and focusing on the process rather than results. More fun and freedom, they surmised, would encourage more dedication to training and build more resilience during matches, which are grueling tests of patience, concentration, and endurance. It's no coincidence that McCullum and Stokes were also two of cricket's great entertainers.

What ensued throughout June and early July was a remarkable turnaround in fortunes. What had changed?

In interviews, Stokes and his teammates spoke about their aspiration to make people fall in love with Test cricket again. Their purpose wasn't just to become the best English cricket team. They wanted to make Test cricket popular and viable, especially given the competition for attention it faced from the much shorter formats. They sought to cross-pollinate skills, introducing some of the more innovative methods of batting and bowling seen in one-day cricket into the five-day Test arena. They hoped to stretch boundaries and challenge tradition.

One of their recipes for success was how McCullum and Stokes created a safe environment for the players. They encouraged players to express themselves more fully, taking risks in pursuit of victory and entertainment, adopting an attacking style of cricket rather than the defensive and unadventurous approach of recent years.

The team also learned to deal more effectively with the fear of failure. When it was clear they would lose against South Africa later that year, they continued to play with a smile on their faces and provide a show for the spectators. A more playful and forgiving culture also sparked a renewed willingness to learn and improve. The culture of Bazball gave the team the resilience to win from behind in extraordinary and record fashion. In all four of their early summer matches against New Zealand and India, the team found themselves batting last, chasing formidable targets that would have tripped them up in the past. They appeared to throw caution to the wind and ultimately emerged victorious, with both established and rookie players thriving in a culture that embraced learning and collaboration. Dolphin leadership had taken the shackles off, made them see what was possible, and inspired them to step out of their comfort zone. By the end of the summer, they had won six of their seven matches. This is testament to what a culture of growth and growth-minded leaders can achieve. Also, Dolphins really are good at cricket.

Refreshing Microsoft

Satya Nadella, CEO of Microsoft and cricket aficionado, would surely appreciate that I chose to follow the story of Bazball with how Nadella went about transforming Microsoft with a growth mindset.

When Nadella succeeded Steve Ballmer as Microsoft's CEO in 2014, he assumed leadership of an organization that appeared to have lost its way. While the company was still profitable under Ballmer, commitment to organizational purpose, customer service, and colleagues had dwindled. Hampered by excessive bureaucracy and internal politics, Microsoft found itself languishing behind innovative tech rivals like Apple, Google, and Facebook. Not only had it floundered in the fields of digital music, search functionality, social networking, e-books, and smart hardware, but it was losing talent as experienced personnel left the company too.

As he explains in *Hit Refresh*, on assuming his new post, Nadella took the opportunity to start over, building on the innovative foundations that had made the company a success in the first place. From the outset, he knew he had to transform Microsoft's culture. In a clear display of Dolphin leadership traits, Nadella wished to place learning and innovation—two of the key elements of a growth mindset—back at the center of the company. Fear of failure, finger-pointing, and endless PowerPoint presentations were replaced with curiosity, responsibility for mistakes, and debate. The company needed people who were *learn-it-alls* rather than *know-it-alls* and could show empathy and care in their dealings with others.

Nadella believes companies grow economically when corporate values connect with deep personal values. This connection allows colleagues to unite in the pursuit of a shared purpose and to subscribe to high levels of personal and organizational integrity. Under Nadella's direction, Microsoft's purpose has centered on "empowering every person and every organization on the planet to achieve more," regardless of which technological field the company is operating in. As Nadella subtitled his book, his championing of cultural change has been motivated by "the quest to rediscover Microsoft's soul and imagine a better future for everyone." In this sense, corporate change needs not only to improve performance but also to bring meaningful benefits to customers and other stakeholders. For example, Microsoft has been helping people with low literacy levels in India by sharing AI-powered applications that can turn speech into text and translate between the country's twenty-one official languages and the two hundred-plus other languages spoken by people living in India.

Nadella also moved Microsoft away from the ultra-competitive and iPhone-smashing approach of Ballmer's era.

He doesn't view competition in rivalrous, zero-sum terms of winners and losers but instead translates it into a driver of excellence: when our competitors are strong, we're pushed to become better ourselves. We learn from rather than undermine or envy others' success. Rather than investing energy in beating the competition, therefore, Microsoft has focused on improving performance and bringing to market products that help its customers. During Nadella's tenure as CEO, Microsoft has sought to build bridges and repair relationships with other organizations, partnering with Apple, Google, and the Linux Foundation, among others. Nadella has referred to these companies as "frenemies," former rivals with whom Microsoft can cooperate to their mutual benefit.

There are many lessons to be learned from Nadella's approach to cultural change and how he integrated growth mindset into how Microsoft innovates. For example, how did he shift Microsoft from resting on its post-Window laurels to becoming one of the most innovative companies in the world in 2023? The answer is commitment.

Commitment

In their 2020 book, *From Incremental to Exponential,* Vivek Wadhwa, Ismail Amla, and Alex Salkever study the ingredients that allow companies, large and small, to innovate. In their review of how culture drives or kills innovation, they argue that "money (increased R&D spending) alone can neither buy innovation nor change corporate culture . . . we have strong evidence that creating an innovation culture, or a culture that encourages and prizes key precursors to innovation, will generate improvements. It is all about focusing on your people. And doing that doesn't cost an arm and a leg." Mindset is a crucial factor in their analysis. They note that the reason

Boeing is struggling to keep up with SpaceX is "a mindset of 'No' as opposed to 'Grow!' All too often, employees in the legacy companies struggle to embrace the new—and so helplessly look on as upstarts blaze new paths that capture their markets by offering greater value." For them, the "spectacular results" achieved by Microsoft illustrate the power of culture to shape innovation through "humility, acceptance for change and openness to external ideas" and by "(dis)organizing for innovation."

The simplicity and insight of that final sentence contrast starkly with the difficulty of leading with a growth mindset and creating a culture for growth. While Wadhwa, Amla, and Salkever offer some important inspiration and suggestions, we need to break down how a growth mindset actually creates better results. To do that, I use the concept of commitment.

Commitment describes a set of attitudes and behaviors that are often referred to as "going the extra mile" (committed to the purpose) and the "intention to stay" (committed to the organization). We associate it with people who do their job well, enjoy it, work well with others, and stay with the team. Leaders who catalyze commitment experience a substantial performance premium in terms of creativity, care, collaboration, and positive customer experiences. They also attract and retain talent. I call this the *commitment premium*.

I prefer the word *commitment* over *employee engagement* because it highlights the choices we all make when it comes to how we work. We choose to perform well, work well with others, and stay. And sometimes we choose to do just enough to avoid attracting attention, work only on our own projects, or leave. We make commitments and break them.

Because commitment is a choice, its biggest enemy is control.

Leaders and organizations naturally tend toward more control, of course. Wadhwa, Amla, and Salkever suggest that we therefore need to "dis(organize)." Innovative cultures don't evolve from scheduling, planning, and mandating innovation. "It does not work on a clock or quarterly calendar; it is not assisted by employee-performance reviews." Nor does it help to have mentoring, coaching, and feedback from experts "higher up in the company" —they simply waste time and perpetuate hierarchies. Instead, "another aid to your internal innovators is to minimize external noise and organizational inertia: to shield them from bureaucracy, meetings, and obligations that are not contributing to their goal; to not mandate performance reviews; and to let them avoid death by review committee."

In Behnam Tabrizi's 2023 HBR article "How Microsoft Became Innovative Again," he provides a deep analysis of the factors that created a "startup mindset" in the company. One of the key factors was reducing hierarchies and freeing engineers from excessive or non-value-adding bureaucracy. The world's largest hackathon became a symbol of an innovative engineering culture let loose and a fabulous opportunity to create nimble networks across hierarchical and professional boundaries.

Control creates unnecessary bureaucracy and friction. Excessive meetings are often a sign of a culture becoming too restrictive. Mandating fewer meetings isn't always the cure. Reviewing and eliminating unnecessary rules (written and unwritten), checks, and controls is a better approach. Dolphins work constantly to reduce and eliminate controlling leadership behaviors, structures, and processes. They also create helpful and healthy processes that provide sensible guardrails and make collaborative work more effective.

Providing opportunities for "random encounters" is a crucial feature of the disorganization that Steve Jobs inspired at Pixar and the Apple campus in Cupertino. So is a bottom-up approach. Wadhwa, Amla, and Salkever write, "The teams need to feel urgency and agency, and to have authority and creativity." They also argue that organizations need to "expect these entrepreneurs and innovators to fly away and launch their own companies . . . taking a restrictive approach to intellectual property will only cause bitterness and will encourage employees to hoard their ideas." Some may stay, others may leave. Both outcomes are good, according to the authors, because they improve your "brand and reputation" and "cement" your culture of innovation. Freedom is critical to innovation. And, as I'll argue below, a key ingredient in a growth mindset.

I often get accused of proposing anarchy. "If we don't control things, there will be chaos," my opponents claim. However, even small choices have a major impact on commitment and performance. If we choose, we perform significantly better than if we only do as we're told. If I tell my daughter to put on "these clothes," she'll fight me. If she gets to choose her clothes, she dresses herself quickly and with a smile.

The latest research on the level of commitment and engagement in US workplaces suggests that most people aren't engaged. According to a 2021 report by Gallup, only 36% of US employees are engaged at work, meaning they're highly involved in and enthusiastic about their work and workplace. Similarly, a 2021 study by the Society for Human Resource Management (SHRM) found that only 38% of US employees reported high levels of job satisfaction, and only 31% reported high levels of engagement. These findings suggest that while organizations have made some progress in improving employee engagement and commitment, there's still significant room for improvement.

Why are employee commitment and engagement so important?

A 2018 study by Gallup found that highly engaged employees are twice as likely as disengaged employees to report having high productivity levels. They also tend to stay in their jobs longer, which reduces turnover costs for companies. The Safe2Great study replicates these findings when it comes to productivity, and found similar correlations with sharing information, quality, and psychological safety.

In 2009, the business writer Daniel Pink wrote *Drive: The Surprising Truth about What Motivates Us*, in which he considers autonomy as central to his Motivation 3.0 theory. "The opposite of autonomy is control. And since they sit at different poles of the behavioral compass, they point us toward different destinations. Control leads to compliance; autonomy leads to engagement." He goes on to cite research involving eleven thousand industrial scientists and engineers that reveals that a desire for intellectual challenge or "the urge to master something new and engaging—was the best predictor of productivity." (You'll find more about this in the Aim High section.) If you only want people to do as they're told, control is fine because your goal is compliance. But if your world is dynamic and requires innovation, and your goal is great, you need commitment.

Why are commitment and engagement so poor?

My research suggests that controlling and cynical leadership are key drivers of lower levels of commitment. The resulting indifference has a reinforcing impact on the workplace culture, which in turn inspires more controlling leadership.

At its most extreme level, this can mean using new technologies to monitor employees. For example, facial recognition technology (FRT), initially applied in law enforcement, uses AI to analyze employees' facial expressions, tone of voice, and other nonverbal cues to assess their emotional state and level of engagement. In the corporate world, FRT is used for security, customer service in hotels and stores, and recruitment.

These technologies are often marketed as tools to help organizations improve employee engagement and productivity. Privacy advocates and labor organizations are alarmed.

Denise Almeida, Konstantin Shmarko, and Elizabeth Lomas of University College London note, "FRT is no longer a topic of science fiction or a concern for the future. It is here now, impacting people's lives on a daily basis, from wrongful arrests to privacy invasions and human rights infringements. The widespread adoption of this technology without appropriate considerations could have catastrophic outcomes."

The negative impact of surveillance on commitment is often referred to as the *panopticon*, denoting eighteenth-century jurist and social reformer Jeremy Bentham's design of a circular prison. When they can't see the prison guard and don't know whether they're being watched or not, Bentham surmised that prisoners would self-regulate their behavior more. It was later used by the French philosopher Michel Foucault in his book *Discipline and Punish: The Birth of the Prison* to describe how modern societies are characterized by surveillance, discipline, and control.

As employment relationships shift to control rather than commitment, the resulting drop in productivity will make it tempting for leaders to use more technology to control effort and measure output. I believe we need to move in the other direction and put technology in the hands of employees. For this to succeed, though, we need leaders with a growth mindset and a willingness to empower people digitally. And we need some healthy corporate regulation.

Boundary spanning

Interdisciplinarity is a feature of innovative cultures. In her book *Hot Spots*, a multi-year study of innovative companies, Lynda Gratton, professor of leadership at London Business School, describes such cultures as boundary spanning and cooperative. She writes: "Leaders who are successful at creating hot spots understand the importance of diversity and inclusion. They recognize that innovation is often driven by the collision of different perspectives and ideas, and they work to create an environment where people from diverse backgrounds and with different experiences can come together to share their knowledge and expertise."

Some years ago, I worked with the leaders of a highly successful, innovative, and interdisciplinary project in the hearing aid industry. The story illustrates the value of the bottom-up approach to commitment. And could easily be called "Alera—when people who know a lot about Bluetooth cell phone technology meet people who know a lot about hearing aids."

In 2008, during the recession, hearing aid manufacturer GN ReSound, owned by GN Store Nord, fell foul of anti-trust regulations. The German courts had ruled against Swiss rival Sonova purchasing GN ReSound, undoing years of preparation. Energy that had been invested in the sale now needed to be redirected toward the creation of a new product line so that the company had something to bring to market. The attention of the product development team therefore turned to the development of a 2.4 gigahertz Bluetooth, directly connected hearing aid. The CEO of a rival company, Oticon, had declared such a device impossible for several technical reasons, not the least the fact that Bluetooth signals struggle to penetrate water—something the brain is full of.

After spending months, including their precious Scandinavian vacation time, on the project, the interdisciplinary team announced success with a wild "we did it" yawp across the atrium of their headquarters in Copenhagen, Denmark. Some years later, the product teams that followed became the first to develop the hardware and software that connected the hearing aid to the iPhone. At the time, the MFI (Made for iPhone) hearing aid was a significant technological breakthrough in audiology, and it paved the way for further GN ReSound innovation and industry leadership over the subsequent decade, including the development of tele-audiology (the remote adjustment of hearing aids to suit the user's unique hearing needs).

By setting themselves the challenge of solving what seemed insoluble (igniting purpose) and showing a strong commitment to the team members (cooperative mindset), the product team was able to puncture organizational, commercial, and academic assumptions; leapfrog geographical boundaries; and create the emotional involvement to explore and discover new possibilities that lay between rather than within their different areas of expertise (boundary spanning). This fusion of three elements—igniting purpose, cooperative mindset, and boundary spanning—resulted in high levels of energy, innovation, and knowledge generation, or what Gratton terms a "hot spot." I say hot spots are driven by commitment, fueled by a growth mindset.

Speaking up reduces screwing up

Organizations that build commitment experience higher quality and improved physical safety. In High Reliability Organizations (HROs), like nuclear power plants and surgical units, it's especially important to foster cultures and leaders with a growth mindset. One particularly interesting example of how HROs operate comes courtesy of the US Navy.

In January 1969, during a battle drill and operational readiness inspection near the Hawaiian island Oahu, a rocket exploded on the flight deck of the USS *Enterprise*. The explosion caused a serious fire and ignited other ordnance, leading to further explosions. Twenty-eight people died and over three hundred were injured. Fatalities could have been higher had it not been for the skillful and timely actions of the medical teams aboard the vessel.

The day-to-day operation of aircraft carriers is complex, risk-filled, and dynamic, with numerous interacting and interdependent parts and functions. Karl Weick's studies of successful and safe operations on these floating oil-covered and saltwater-encrusted airfields no bigger than football fields emphasize the importance of "heedful interactions" (i.e., psychological safety) in dangerous work environments. That there have been few incidents among US Navy carriers since the *Enterprise* explosion is testament to an organizational culture where people strive to explain, question, and learn every day in their quest for reliability and safety.

Yet the hallmark of an HRO isn't that it's error-free but that it learns from errors and staff are always on the alert for unusual or unprecedented threats. Normally, we associate learning with stable teams, but the US Navy operates within the framework of a temporary crew who are rotated on and off the ship every four months. The system works because there's a strong learning culture in which specialist petty officers take responsibility for developing competence and maintaining excellence. By practicing constant training and retraining, they keep their crews focused, maintain a reliable flow of information and knowledge, and build resilience within and between teams. It's vital that the organizational culture is one in which individuals and teams can interact with and challenge each other respectfully, and where expertise carries more weight than hierarchical rank.

Despite what some of my clients think, mistakes happen every day, and leaders miss opportunities every day. Of course, leaders shouldn't encourage mistakes as a way to improve quality. Rather, they must reduce the fear of revealing and discussing mistakes and ways to avoid repeating them. Safe2Great advocates "speak up," not "screw up more."

However, organizations with big differences in status or other types of hierarchies are more likely to experience a conspiracy of silence. My research shows that organizations high on controlling and cynical leadership have considerably lower levels of psychological safety and report higher levels of senior leaders taking a cavalier approach to health and safety regulations.

It's telling, therefore, that whether they're in a military setting, at a nuclear power plant, or doing surgery, growth-minded leaders create the safe relationships that allow those they lead to speak up. When team members stop caring about or noticing unusual or unexpected data, the chances of a dangerous or major negative event increase. "It's not what you know that kills you on an oil rig," a client in the drilling industry said to me during a coaching session. "It's what has never happened before that gets people killed or badly hurt."

Deep empathy

The COVID-19 pandemic revealed to all of us how important hospitals and other health-care providers are to our well-being and survival. It also revealed that we're struggling, even in countries with well-funded health care like Denmark, to keep up with human needs and the possibilities of modern medicine. If we want life-enhancing and life-saving treatments to be universally accessible, we need to invest increasing amounts of money in health care—including the people who provide that care.

The health-care sector is a significant employer in most OECD economies. According to Dr. Eric Topol, cardiologist and expert in the future of medicine, "Healthcare became not just a big business, by the end of 2017, the biggest. It is now the largest employer in the United States, towering over retail." Health care employs more than 16 million people and accounts for 18% of US GDP. It's become big business, but it's also become dehumanized. For example, the time spent on each patient has fallen from sixty minutes on average in 1975, to twelve minutes in 2019. Furthermore, workers in health care are suffering from commitment overload.

According to Topol, medicine lags almost all other industries in terms of technological innovation. And that's hurting the people who work in that sector. If data was digitized and made available across platforms, health-care providers and researchers could use the deep learning potential of AI to revolutionize diagnosis, prognosis, drug development, and patient care. In addition to increasing speed and accuracy and reducing costs, AI could allow doctors to individualize diagnoses and treatment with genome and proteome level insights, although Topol recognizes that data protection will be a key aspect of success in this area. On a more human level, he notes that "what's wrong in healthcare today is that it's missing care." He believes AI represents the best opportunity to "restore the precious and time-honored connection and trust–the human touch–between patients and doctors." Corobotics can make deep empathy possible. It could also go a long way to addressing the rates of burnout and mental health issues among health-care providers by allowing them to improve their impact. If, that is, we choose to put people first.

When people have a bigger impact they're more committed. But when work becomes inhuman, they become cynical–the second biggest enemy of commitment. When even our best efforts aren't enough to get the job done, we stop believing in what we're doing. Stress and burnout follow.

Ecosystems

The accepted wisdom used to be that going in circles was a bad thing. Today, circularity is a key strategy for the Green Age. It also demands a new type of commitment.

In general, a circular economy depends on the use of renewable materials–the ability to regenerate, restore, repair, reuse, refurbish, or recycle–and the minimal loss of both materials and energy. It's aligned with the idea of moving from mining to farming.

The Danish pharmaceutical company Novo Nordisk aims to generate zero carbon dioxide emissions from its operations and transport by 2030 and to achieve net zero emissions across all areas of business by 2045. Circular for Zero commits Novo Nordisk to discovering new ways to design recyclable and reusable products, minimize consumption and waste, and work with suppliers who share the company's sustainable objectives. It's a bold ambition for an organization that currently uses huge quantities of water and energy to manufacture and distribute medicines, vials, and injection pens—but it's essentially more achievable compared to what other companies must change to achieve circularity.

In other industries, products must become part of other circular businesses. Danfoss, for example, is a global Danish manufacturing company working in climate solutions (heating and cooling), electric drives, and power solutions. For them, achieving circularity is about finding ways to work toward green solutions with their customers, their customers' customers, governments, and consumers. This requires an emerging ecosystem approach to leadership which challenges how they—and we—think about commitment.

As leading and partnering across the ecosystem will be essential in the Green Age, leaders will have to show commitment to a common purpose that arches across companies, governments, suppliers, and consumers. We'll need visions and strategies that inspire and mobilize more than employees. In a 2022 HBR article titled "Today's CEOs Don't Just Lead Companies. They Lead Ecosystems," the researchers Sarah Jensen Clayton, Tiernay Remick, and Evelyn Orr write that "86% of CEOs and board members see business and society becoming more interconnected, and two thirds of the American public want CEOs to take a stand on social issues." They argue that CEOs will need "a different type of CEO: an enterprise leader who also stewards the ecosystem in which their business operates, including customers, suppliers, partners, competitors, governments, and their local community."

Michael Jacobides, professor of strategy at London Business School, writes in a 2019 HBR article that "in ecosystem competition, success is as much about helping other firms innovate as it is about being innovative yourself." There are many choices to make when determining your ecosystem strategy—for example, whether to be the orchestrator or complementor of an ecosystem—but no matter what strategy you choose, he argues that "competing is increasingly about identifying new ways to collaborate and connect rather than simply offering alternative value propositions."

I believe this trend toward ecosystem leadership means that commitment is no longer to companies but to purposes that transcend any individual company. This is especially true for organizational members. If you want to attract talented people, you'll need to realign your own organization toward the purpose of an ecosystem rather than your company's financial success.

My Safe2Great research has shown me that when leaders and organizations make commitments to causes and purposes that go beyond profit and contribute to ecosystems, and deliver on them, their people demonstrate higher commitment. But you have to be sincere. Employees know too much to be easily fooled by smart marketing and spin. Whenever the gap between reality and the story becomes too great, cynicism results. And cynicism is more contagious than commitment.

Summary

Because the Globotic Age will threaten autonomy and choice profoundly, leaders will have to create a different kind of commitment. There will be no commitment to learn, collaborate, or innovate if we don't reduce the threats, mitigate the losses, and increase the equity of how the benefits of AI are distributed. We need to hand over the keys to the smart machines to our employees. In their hands, we have a better chance of improving safety, equity, and opportunity. If we don't, we risk rebellion or worse, caustic cynicism.

Leaders who subscribe to the growth mindset principles will catalyze the commitment premium by creating more autonomous, resilient, and creative people and teams than those who don't. Their teams will pay greater attention to details, take more risks, experiment and innovate more, and work more effectively with others. They'll integrate AI and robotics into their work practices to enhance productivity and make work more manageable. They'll also participate more actively and respectfully in communities inside, outside, and across the organization, positively affecting the circulation of ideas, level of engagement, and quality of service delivery throughout the organization.

In the next chapters, I present my six growth principles in detail. They might look obvious or simple, but effective solutions don't need to be complex. Sometimes it pays to keep things simple. And sometimes, what looks simple from the outside is actually challenging to put into action. The principles are designed to take all the lessons I've written about so far and turn them into memorable, actionable, and measurable practices. They're an important framework for starting your growth mindset journey, helping others grow, and creating cultures for growth.

2

Transform

How can we make the work we do and the changes we make more meaningful?

Overview

Great leadership really does start with a dream.

Transform was one of the most important elements I wanted to include in the Safe2Great Growth Mindset model. And I'm glad I did. When I studied the results of our Growth Mindset Leadership 360 and Culture for Growth assessments, it was clear to me that leaders and cultures that demonstrated the behaviors associated with Transform were correlated with significantly higher levels of effectiveness, commitment, and psychological safety. In fact, from a statistical perspective, it's true to say that people perform best when they have a strong "why." And today the why is changing in business from making a company financially successful to other goals like saving the planet.

The Transform principle includes practices like communicating a bold vision, defining a strong purpose, and role-modeling integrity and service to customers and communities. It's one of the pillars on which the commitment premium rests. When leaders Transform, team members feel that they're serving a purpose that goes beyond short-term profit or personal gratification. They're making a meaningful and positive impact on other people and working with others toward a common purpose. They feel they belong to a community. It not only creates commitment but also stimulates ethical and responsible behavior.

Transforming leaders and cultures create the conditions in which people are willing to compromise and collaborate to benefit the customer, community, or environment, rather than optimize their own needs or position. This can only happen if we connect people across organizational silos and cultural boundaries, establishing common purposes and shared aspirations. Transforming leaders unite the personal and the communal, aligning individual and organizational purposes and goals in a way that creates sustainable and ethical outcomes. A common purpose makes it possible for teams and organizations to be more than the sum of their parts.

When we Transform, we harness the relational potential of our people not only to help our families, colleagues, and community, but also to do good for the environment, wider ecology, and future generations. To Transform is to create synergies, not internal competition. It means to acknowledge and atone for the errors of the past, deliver in the present, and steward the future for our children, grandchildren, and beyond. To Transform is to become the change you want to be in the world.

Benefits

· Inspires change with a bold vision.
· Creates a strong sense of common purpose.
· Incorporates sustainability into problem-solving.
· Breaks down silos.

Skolstrejk för Klimatet

The climate activist Greta Thunberg discovered her purpose at a young age, and it's one that aligned with a higher purpose on a global level. Initially, though, she was overwhelmed by the contradictions of modern life. Having been shown a documentary at school about the climate crisis but seeing how little people were doing about it, she became depressed, stopped eating, and elected to talk only to her parents, sister, and pet dogs—if she spoke at all.

Thunberg has Asperger syndrome, high-functioning autism, and obsessive-compulsive disorder. She viewed the climate issue in terms of black and white, right and wrong, and empty words and effective action. She witnessed the failures of world leaders and everyday citizens in the face of an accelerating crisis and despaired for the future.

At home, Thunberg started working on her family, arguing that they should change their consumerist lifestyle, stop eating meat, and never travel by aircraft, using trains, boats, and electric cars instead, to do their bit to reduce emissions. Slowly, as they all adapted, she began to eat again, engage with others online, and educate herself with laser-like focus and near-photographic recall about climate-related science. She was re-energized, ready to act and to try to make a difference.

With the Parliamentary election cycle under way in 2018, fifteen-year-old Thunberg realized that none of the political parties in Sweden were engaging meaningfully with the climate crisis. This should have been the most pressing issue of the day, given that there was so little time left to implement policies to achieve the 2015 Paris Agreement mitigation targets before the situation spiraled completely out of control. Thunberg could now make a stand, putting her purpose into action with her first public display of activism.

For three weeks, starting on August 20, 2018, and ending on September 9, the day of the elections, Thunberg sat outside the Swedish Parliament with a hand-painted sign that declared "Skolstrejk för Klimatet" (school strike for the climate). The schoolgirl, who had until recently been traumatized by bullying and rarely spoke, interacted freely with passersby and the media in both Swedish and English, distributed her carefully compiled factsheets, and explained the stance she was taking and why she believed it was necessary.

When the first young person sat down next to Thunberg to join her on the street, a movement was born. When the elections were over, Thunberg announced the launch of the Fridays For Future protests, inviting others to accompany her in continuing to raise awareness and push for action that properly addressed the threat of climate breakdown and mass extinction. The protests soon became a global phenomenon. In September 2019, more than 7 million people across the world went on strike for the climate.

Thunberg has mobilized and inspired many others, particularly young people, to protest inaction on climate issues. She has relied on science rather than rhetoric, and spoken truth to power without subterfuge, smokescreens, or caveats when invited to address institutional gatherings or meet with political leaders. With a clarity of argument and delivery well beyond her years, she speaks candidly and boldly—almost brutally—to people much older than her and with significantly more life and work experience, highlighting the responsibilities of those currently holding power and the devastating legacy they're leaving for future generations.

In 2019, Thunberg traveled by yacht to New York City to attend the UN Climate Action Summit. Her "How Dare You?" speech, constructed around a challenging and igniting question, quickly went viral, discomforting attendees as she laid bare distressing truths in crystal-clear terms.

> You have stolen my dreams and my childhood with your empty words. And yet I'm one of the lucky ones. People are suffering. People are dying. Entire ecosystems are collapsing. And all you can talk about is money and fairy tales of eternal economic growth. How dare you?
>
> For more than thirty years, the science has been crystal clear. How dare you continue to look away and come here saying that you're doing enough, when the politics and solutions needed are still nowhere in sight?

Purpose

Common purpose is at the heart of all complex and committed effort. When people have a clear, inspiring, and uniting challenge to solve, they can achieve the highest levels of performance, collaboration, and innovation. When they believe in what they do and its positive impact on the world, they become more resilient, hopeful, and resourceful.

All of Lynda Gratton's hot spots had an *igniting purpose*, a shared sense of meaning and direction that inspires and motivates people to work together toward a common goal. This purpose isn't just about financial or strategic goals. It's also about making a positive impact on the world and creating a sense of fulfillment and meaning for those involved. She writes: "In a productive Hot Spot, there has to be a point of ignition. It is at this point that all the latent energy contained within the cooperative mindset and the cross-boundary working is released."

In his extensive review of this subject in the book *Deep Purpose*, Harvard professor Ranjay Gulati notes that there is a qualitative difference between an instrumental purpose and deep purpose. Companies that truly ignite their teams and all their stakeholders use their purpose to shape everything they do. Blackrock, Unilever, and Patagonia, for example, all demonstrate that a compelling purpose has two features: "First, they delineate an ambitious, longer-term goal for the company. Second, they give this goal an idealistic cast, committing the firm to fulfillment of broader social duties."

Daniel Pink writes about the difference between the *profit motive* and the *purpose motive* in *Drive*: "Autonomous people working toward mastery perform at very high levels. But those who do so in the service of some greater objective can achieve even more." In ecosystems, a purpose enables the kind of cross-company and multi-stakeholder approach necessary in the Green Age.

Novo Nordisk's Defeat Diabetes social responsibility strategy, for example, represents a bold aspiration and a strong sense of purpose. If you're one of the world's largest insulin manufacturers, it can seem self-defeating or disingenuous at first glance to reduce your target market. But it depends on how you deliver on your promise. Novo Nordisk was one of the first companies to implement the triple bottom line, so it's not surprising that they now push their impact beyond purely treating diseases to also curing them or eliminating their debilitating symptoms.

In his book *The Purpose Effect,* adjunct professor Dan Pontefract quotes from an interview with Aaron Hurst, the author of *The Purpose Economy*: "Creating a successful organization in the Purpose Economy requires two types of leadership. You need authentic leaders who are able to model purpose and vulnerability and you need leaders who have the courage to look beyond short-term results."

The biggest challenge in terms of purpose in the corporate world is the gap between words and deeds. When people observe greenwashing, it creates cynicism. Leaders must live their message, demonstrating accountability and making big commitments.

Thunberg managed to do this successfully. Her uncompromising commitment to the cause has proven extraordinarily contagious. It's a hard act to follow in the corporate world, but I think it's the only way forward.

Transform guidance

- Use an igniting question to establish a bold vision for the future.
- Break barriers by connecting people across the organization regardless of role, status, or team hierarchy.
- Incorporate sustainable and ethical principles into every aspect of the business.
- Build a community rather than a company that stretches across boundaries, bringing together employees, customers, suppliers, and owners.
- Leave your private jet at home and take the bus.

3

Aim High

How do we create a pathway to achieve our vision that balances risk and ambition in a sustainable, motivating, and participative way?

Overview

Aim High is essentially the desire to do better. For a leader, it's about creating a pathway and developing the methods to realize vision and purpose. To paraphrase Antoine de Saint-Exupéry, a vision without a plan is just wishful thinking. Great leadership rests on the ability to plan well and the ability to manage resources effectively. These skills are also two of the most important drivers of great outcomes in the Safe2Great surveys. When they Aim High, leaders set challenging, meaningful, and achievable goals together with their staff, or let them set their own goals. Balancing autonomy and responsibility is one of the key challenges of Aim High. It can be achieved by providing ways for people to (self-)monitor their progress toward goals while simultaneously allowing for self-direction in their accomplishment.

Aim High is about mastery, and its language is based on facts rather than fads.

Aim High is about using external data and information to stimulate people to learn and improve; and providing scoreboards so that team members go home each day feeling like they've made progress. It's about creating healthy processes that provide important guardrails and allow for the unexpected; and developing organizing principles that stimulate fast collaboration and rapid prototyping across functions. It's about building a constructive bureaucracy based on smart rules—not rules for every interaction, just those that have the biggest positive impact—and creating a transparent organizational political environment that stimulates participation, equity, and accountability.

When leaders Aim High, they adopt practices that drive excellence in quality and performance. There are strong connections here to thinking in other popular frameworks like Agile and Lean. Aim High is about being participative, being reasonable about risk and ambition, and constantly looking for external evidence for decisions and feedback on results.

Benefits

· Stimulates intrinsic motivators like mastery and autonomy.
· Promotes transparency and fairness, informed by data and analysis.
· Shifts accountability and responsibility downward.
· Creates the optimal level of challenge and risk-taking.

Fail safe

Space and the stars have long confounded and fascinated scientists, philosophers, mythologists, authors, explorers, and engineers in equal measure. The second half of the twentieth century was marked by the successes and discoveries of the Soviet Sputnik and Vostok programs and the National Aeronautics and Space Administration (NASA) Apollo and Space Shuttle missions. And more recently, the endeavors of private enterprises like Amazon and SpaceX, backed by high-profile, wealthy investors such as Jeff Bezos and Elon Musk, have reignited public interest in space travel and exploration.

In many respects, the 1960s witnessed some of the most significant breakthroughs of the Space Age, bookended by Soviet cosmonaut Yuri Gagarin's first orbit of Earth in April 1961 and US astronaut Neil Armstrong's first steps on the moon in July 1969. The latter's "giant leap" for humankind might not have been possible, however, without the work of Margaret Hamilton and her coding team at the Massachusetts Institute of Technology's (MIT) Instrumentation Laboratory. Hamilton was director of the Software Engineering Division, which was responsible for the Apollo mission's guidance system for command and lunar landing vehicles.

Occasionally, Hamilton's daughter Lauren would accompany her to the Instrumentation Lab while she worked on the guidance system. During one visit, Lauren inadvertently launched a simulated mission, then activated a prelaunch program. This erased navigation data and caused the "mission" to fail. The mishap provided invaluable insights for Hamilton. If an astronaut were to enter the incorrect command code, erasing navigation data, it might be impossible for them to return to Earth.

Hamilton escalated the issue, recommending a software override that would maintain the integrity of the navigation system. But she was informed by the NASA hierarchy that "astronauts don't make mistakes" and that there was no possibility of such a mistake being reproduced on a real mission.

Unconvinced, and perhaps a little frustrated with her all-male leadership team, she included an advisory note in the system documentation. Sure enough, during the moon-orbiting *Apollo 8* mission in December 1968, astronaut Jim Lovell entered the same command code as Lauren had, with the same drastic effect.

It fell to Hamilton and her colleagues to create a fix that could be uploaded to *Apollo 8* via Mission Control, enabling the crew's safe return. Following this narrow escape from disaster, Hamilton was permitted to create the fail-safe code that she'd previously advocated. Her code for a priority display system later proved life-saving during the moon-landing phase of the *Apollo 11* mission.

Seven and a half minutes from landing on the moon, the lunar module's guidance computer began to ring a bell and flash 1202. Neither Armstrong nor Buzz Aldrin, the pilots on the *Eagle*, the lunar module, had ever seen this error code in their extensive simulations. Back on Earth, the flight surgeons captured the rapid increase in the astronauts' heart rate. Ground Control didn't have an immediate answer. Initially they hoped it was an insignificant glitch.

"We're go on that alarm," responded Charlie Duke, who was in the capcom seat at Ground Control that day. With years of test pilot work in prototype aircraft at the edge of the atmosphere and more than twice the speed of sound, Armstrong and Aldrin had learned to trust their team. If they were go, they were go. So even though the system continued to reboot, ring, and flash 1202 and now also 1201, they continued to focus on finding a safe place to land the *Eagle*. They were nowhere near their original landing site. They had other things to worry about, like running out of fuel or landing on a rock. And death.

They learned later that the error was due to the switch for the rendezvous radar being set for docking rather than landing. That caused the radar to send lots of irrelevant data to the guidance computer and overload its tiny memory. Luckily, Hamilton and her team had foreseen this problem. They had designed the system to fail safe. When overloaded, the guidance computer would rapidly reboot to empty the memory and thus allow the system to manage the important stuff like height and speed. The crew landed with only seventeen seconds of fuel left on the gauge. Actually, they had forty-five seconds of fuel left, because the gauge was reading wrong.

In 2009, Hamilton and several of her colleagues from the space program were interviewed by MIT News to mark the fortieth anniversary of the lunar landing. Reflecting on her experiences of the Apollo missions and the culture that prevailed at MIT and NASA at the time, she observed:

> Coming up with solutions and new ideas was an adventure. Dedication and commitment were a given. Mutual respect was across the board. Because software was a mystery, a black box, upper management gave us total freedom and trust. We had to find a way and we did. Looking back, we were the luckiest people in the world; there was no choice but to be pioneers; no time to be beginners.

Autonomy

In *Escape from Freedom*, the philosopher and psychologist Erich Fromm distinguishes between two types of freedom: freedom *from* and freedom *to*. Fromm had fled Nazi Germany, emigrating to the United States and experiencing freedom from an oppressive and murderous regime. Conversely, during her work on the Apollo missions, Hamilton enjoyed self-determination and the freedom to explore and innovate, reveling in the autonomy afforded her by MIT's Instrumentation Laboratory. (Except when her male colleagues thought they knew better.)

In *Mastering Community*, Christine Porath writes that building communities that create real change requires autonomy, or what she refers to as *unleashing*, "the intentional loss of control of thousands of creative people who are moving in the direction of a desired goal."

According to Daniel Pink, people who have autonomy and the desire to master their work develop practices like data collection, feedback, self-discipline, and ownership of both positive and negative outcomes. They ask questions, seek improvements, and work with others to develop and enhance, rather than simply continuing to do the same things in the same way because that's how they've always been done. Mastery requires openness and honesty, responding to what the data tells us, putting in place the infrastructure and feedback processes that facilitate progress.

Aim High isn't a free-for-all. It's an optimal balance between autonomy and process-discipline; between ambitious goals and available resources; between risk-taking and doing what we know works. People work best together when they have enabling rules, a playing field, roles, techniques, and scoreboards but also the freedom to explore and experiment within their bounds, and perhaps to change the rules themselves.

In many respects Aim High is about creating a system that's independent of the leader—a flexible, psychologically safe framework within which people can operate without the constraints of absolute control or someone constantly peering over their shoulders and can develop and apply their own experience, blend their knowledge with that of others, assess risks, make collective decisions and act on them, and share lessons learned.

Autonomy can release extraordinary levels of performance and ingenuity, with results often outpacing deadlines and delivering above expectations. That's why it's important for leaders to help nurture the conditions in which employees feel encouraged to step forward and take ownership and account-ability. Leaders also need to know when to get out of the way. Otherwise, self-direction and self-efficacy dwindle exponen-tially. There's such a thing as too much leadership, when peo-ple stop thinking and acting of their own accord and wait to be told what to do. I discuss this in more detail in The Dark Side.

Aim High guidance

· Have a clear set of goals and expectations that create a positive stretch.
· Use data to assess current performance and ideas.
· Create a scoreboard to monitor progress.
· Work in a structured and disciplined way to achieve goals.
· Let your child play with your computer.

4

Explore

How can we foster teams and organizations that regularly consider new ways of working, new ideas, and new perspectives?

Overview

Satya Nadella expressed his desire to have Microsoft filled with learn-it-alls rather than know-it-alls. This is the essence of Explore. Great teams and curious leaders remain open to ideas, whether they're sourced from within or outside their organizations. They're willing to examine alternative ways of doing things, consider facts that disrupt current thinking, subject their own blind spots to scrutiny, and experiment and play. They're newsmart.

Explore is about directing our learning toward what's out there; being open to new experiences; and better understanding the world, our organizations, and ourselves. It requires us to seek out and provide challenging feedback; to follow our curiosity, endeavoring to learn more when we encounter something new; to treat our mistakes like our successes, acknowledging and embracing them, learning from and sharing them, and finding the humor in them.

As behavioral scientist Jennifer Aaker and corporate strategist Naomi Bagdonas demonstrate in their book, *Humour, Seriously*, playfulness and a willingness to find humor even in failure help people overcome fear, develop strong relationships with their colleagues, and foster a creative environment. *Humour, Seriously* is a bestseller, but I've yet to see humor used as best practice in organizations. There's something profoundly taboo about making fun of your business, your products, your leaders, and especially your customers. It can also be very expensive. Gerald Ratner drove his business almost to ruin after he made fun of some of its products in a speech in 1991. The Ratner group lost GBP500 million, and Ratner was kicked out of the company he founded. "Doing a Ratner," even when no one is watching and you've confiscated all the cell phones, is a bad idea. There's no role for the court jester, it seems.

Emotional engagement with others—both playful and serious—leads to a free flow of ideas and knowledge exchange. Curiosity about other perspectives can result in innovation and new insights, unlocking potential, improving practice, and creating breakthroughs. When we Explore, it's easy to share ideas, challenges, and solutions. Explore builds bonds between people, bridging artificial divides and bringing them together to create, solve problems, and take advantage of opportunities, pushing the boundaries of what's known and what's possible. We saw this in the collaboration between NASA and MIT's Instrumentation Laboratory. We'll see it again with Pixar.

Benefits

· Encourages experimentation and learning.
· Stimulates creativity and innovation.
· Enables people to seek feedback, share problems, and challenge openly.
· Creates a culture in which errors are a source of learning rather than a cause for blame.

Monsters Inc.

Ed Catmull was one of the co-founders of Pixar Animation Studios and a president of Walt Disney Animation Studios. In a 2008 *HBR* article—and then in greater detail in his 2014 book, *Creativity, Inc.*, co-authored with Amy Wallace—Catmull explains how he considered it his role as an organizational leader to cultivate an environment in which others could flourish and realize more fully their creative capabilities and potential. As a member of the Pixar leadership triumvirate along with Steve Jobs and John Lasseter, Catmull sought to introduce practices and communities that could enable his colleagues to Explore in a safe environment.

From early on, numerous initiatives were implemented to encourage learning, knowledge-sharing, and feedback. These included the design of the Pixar headquarters themselves, which were constructed in such a way that employees would inevitably have "random" encounters with colleagues from other departments and functions. Meeting rooms, bathrooms, mailboxes, and the cafeteria were all located in a central atrium. This was a form of engineered "serendipity," the apocryphal water cooler on a grand scale.

Explore also informed the establishment of Pixar University, which was about learning together and having fun doing so. The courses on offer encouraged staff to be curious about the skills and methods used in other areas of the business, whether technical or creative, fostering empathy for colleagues in other departments. In addition, staff could study exercise methods, not only to benefit their health but also to gain a greater understanding of how the human body moves. This new knowledge was used to improve how the animated figures moved on screen.

One of the most productive Explore practices at Pixar, however, was the company's approach to peer reviews and feedback, both constructive and critical. These took various forms and were refined over time as Catmull and his peers learned the importance of establishing psychological safety so that people could be candid with one another and not over-protective of or sensitive about their work. They aspired to an environment of collective learning and improvement.

Filmmakers, for example, had to preview their work in progress, showing dailies, however rough and ready they might be. They could also seek feedback and suggestions for improvement from a "brains trust" composed of senior directors, producers, and executives. Each film would also be subjected to a post-production postmortem, the format of which would change movie by movie to ensure that what was learned was valuable rather than formulaic. This was a speak-up environment with high cultural and quality expectations.

Feedback, peer review, and constructive support were intended to help directors, writers, animators, and technicians, all of whom contributed to film production, the creative process, and the company's knowledge base. Candid exchanges of views and occasional moments of creative friction reflected an organizational culture founded on notions of learning and growth rather than on any desire to compete or belittle. Pixar wanted to avoid becoming stuck and complacent. Leaders like Catmull knew that if the company stood still, basking in its current success, it faced the prospect of long-term irrelevance and decline.

Interviewed for the *McKinsey Quarterly* in 2008, the writer and director Brad Bird recalled being challenged by Catmull, Jobs, and Lasseter to shake things up when he joined Pixar in 2000. They wanted him to push his colleagues to continue to Explore, to never rest on their laurels. But they warned him that he should expect a good argument if he couldn't convince his peers of the viability of alternative methods and approaches.

Bird took their challenge to heart. Initially, he worked with the company's "misfits" to push the envelope of what was possible technically and financially in animated feature films. The result was the hit movie *The Incredibles*. Bird then moved on to rescue *Ratatouille*, which had been floundering for some time. He not only achieved a technical breakthrough by questioning the underlying premise for how the cast of rats should be animated, but also tightened the storyline by identifying what motivated the protagonist and why. His intervention illustrated how technical and creative lines can be blurred by the desire to Explore.

Curiosity

Before he joined Pixar, Bird worked in other animation studios, including Disney's. In the *McKinsey* interview, he recalls with reverence the old guard of Disney animators that he encountered. What he learned from them was a perfect fit for the culture at Pixar: "They were masters of the form, but they had the attitude of a student." Curiosity, as these master animators demonstrated, is one of the most important characteristics of people who contribute positively to innovative and creative organizations. People who innovate learn about many different things, giving them the fuel to challenge existing ideas or to combine them in unusual ways. They read, they research, they practice, and they work with people who are masters in their field. They discover gaps in knowledge and dive in to find out what lies at the bottom. They are open to experience and can suspend judgment, at least long enough to find out why things work the way they do. They're confident in their own ability to learn, and their willingness to cast off old ideas and habits in search of new or better ways makes them highly adaptable.

People who are curious and creative learn to tolerate their own bad ideas as they move toward coming up with better ones. More importantly, from the perspective of their own teams and organizations, they can tolerate less-than-perfect ideas from others. They know that coming up with ideas and sharing them is the way to practice innovation, and that new ideas, and the people who own them, are fragile and sensitive, easily damaged by mockery or destructive criticism. That's why movies remain unmade, space missions remain on the ground, products remain undeveloped, problems remain unsolved, and new knowledge remains untapped. And of course, why great books remain unwritten.

Curious and innovative people are like gymnasts learning to tumble and twist. They need a soft place to crash-land, a big fat mat on which to soften the ego blow of criticism. They need to test out ideas, however left-field and bizarre, with their peers. This allows them to experiment and investigate, discovering new pathways to improvement and success. At Pixar, interaction with the brains trust and regular feedback sessions after the screening of dailies translated into a series of Academy Awards, numerous technological patents, and a healthy bottom line, which funded yet more exploration. Explore really is the principle closest in spirit to Carol Dweck's concept of growth mindset.

Explore guidance

· Ask for and act on feedback from others.

· Have fun and play.

· Be humble socially and cognitively.

· Suspend judgment and open your mind.

· Never underestimate a French rat.

5

Go High

How can we use our energy and emotions to shape positive thinking, confidence, and decisive action in the face of setbacks and failures?

Overview

Go High is about presence, resilience, calmness, and thinking clearly under pressure. It's a crucial aspect of growth-minded leadership because, when faced with complex situations, emergencies, and tragedies, we often experience cognitive overload and stress, exacerbated by the needs of all the different people we need to work with and support (collaborative overload). When leaders Go High, they retain the ability to positively influence others and to gain commitment while others lose their heads and start bossing people around.

When we Go High, we circumvent strong negative emotions and maintain clarity of thought. That allows us to make good decisions, engage effectively with those around us, and focus on the most important thing to do or discuss. We can then ensure that energy is directed toward positive and constructive outcomes, and that we recover from setbacks rather than becoming immersed in self-pity or anger.

Leaders who Go High find opportunities and solutions even as they navigate and resolve problems others consider insoluble. They're optimistic, tempered with a dash of realism. They demonstrate emotional resourcefulness, even in highly unpleasant or tense situations. Theirs is a cup-half-full perspective, and it informs the teams they lead and how they and their colleagues respond to fresh challenges. By communicating clearly, sincerely, and respectfully—even when conveying difficult news—they can bring others with them.

In essence, Go High is about how we show up in every meeting and every conversation at work. Leaders set the emotional tone of a meeting even before they say a word. And thinking follows emotion. We shape our thinking in response to how we feel. Threatened, we prepare to defend ourselves or run. Angry, we act out our frustrations with rude or intimidating language. Inspired, we share and commit our ideas and enthusiasm to a common goal. Many workplaces today have too much indifference, impatience, and anger. None of these emotions provide a good environment for collaboration, psychological safety, or growth. Go High is the emotional key to unlock relational potential and commitment.

Benefits
· Builds resilience and energy in the team.
· Maintains people's attention and focus during critical moments.
· Prevents frustration and disappointment from becoming blame and conflict.
· Helps to make people approachable during conflicts.

Christchurch

During afternoon prayers on March 15, 2019, a lone gunman opened fire in Christchurch, New Zealand, first in the Al Noor mosque, then in the Linwood Islamic Centre. Brenton Harrison Tarrant, a white supremacist Australian national with links to the alt-right, live-streamed his actions as he slaughtered fifty-one people and injured forty others.

Methodical and premeditated, Tarrant's terrorist attack echoed those of the anti-Islam militant Anders Breivik, on Utøya island in Norway in July 2011, and the neo-Nazi Dylann Roof, who murdered a group of African American people attending Bible study at a church in Charleston, South Carolina, in June 2015. Tarrant's was the most significant act of terrorism on New Zealand soil in the modern era.

In the immediate aftermath of the attacks, New Zealand's prime minister at the time, Jacinda Ardern, visited Muslim communities in Christchurch and other cities, demonstrating empathy and care for the people she met, while condemning the actions and ideology of the killer. Wearing a black hijab as a mark of respect, she hugged people affected by the tragedy and whispered private words of condolence to them. Her compassionate, authentic, and unselfconscious interactions contrasted markedly with those of other world leaders in similarly tragic circumstances.

Ardern's actions were grounded in establishing genuine human connection rather than scoring political points. Her concern was with helping a targeted community—and the nation as a whole—express its grief while retaining the resilience to withstand the threat posed to its way of life by extremists. She sought to include rather than separate, refusing to name the killer and insisting that the names of the victims be voiced. "New Zealand mourns with you," she declared. "We are one." At prayers a week after the shooting, the imam of Al Noor mosque responded, "We are broken-hearted, but we are not broken."

Ardern's leadership at this time displayed something central to the idea of Going High. She showed steeliness and courage, remaining connected to others through empathy, presence, and openness. Her emotional availability not only helped the victims but also sent a strong message to all New Zealanders—and communities across the world—about the strength of care and moral integrity even in the face of existential threats. In the wake of the massacre, she created a powerful political and social force built on community and compassion, which was backed up with the right messaging and followed swiftly with practical measures, such as new gun legislation enacted weeks after the tragedy.

Significantly, Ardern didn't force people to do as she did. Instead, many ordinary New Zealanders followed her lead and chose community and compassion over self-interest and suspicion. Ardern also made the personal choice to meet widespread cynicism and hate with care and empathy. She showed more grit than growl.

Grit

In her study of grit, the psychologist Angela Duckworth argues that those who experience success tend to combine passion with perseverance, and determination with direction. Jacinda Ardern's behavior after the attack on the mosque illustrates how emotional resilience—the grit to stay alert, resourceful, and clear-headed when facing adversity—is the key to leading in a crisis and why it's at the heart of the Go High operating mode. With grit, we never give up. We recover from disaster and learn from what went wrong, correcting mistakes or, as Margaret Hamilton did, implementing fail-safes.

Robert Sutton comments in *Good Boss, Bad Boss*, "Great bosses instill grit in followers. They are dogged and patient, pressing themselves and others to move ever forward. Gritty bosses create urgency without treating life as one long emergency." Anger, authoritarianism, indecision, and an unwillingness to listen to or engage with others all undermine a leader's strategy and cause often irreparable harm. Being growth-minded rather than self-protective is a better strategy when facing extraordinary circumstances.

Disasters usually arise in unusual, unexpected, or unpredictable circumstances. The mosque shootings, the explosion aboard the USS *Enterprise*, and the COVID-19 pandemic aren't everyday events. In the context of disasters, existing solutions and strategies may be unsuccessful or irrelevant. In some cases, they make things worse.

Grit requires us to persevere as we assess possible remedies and responses, interacting heedfully with colleagues and partners, sense-making continuously as new data and knowledge become available. How we interpret a situation or crisis shapes our decisions and actions. We must trust in the expertise of others, sharing frankly and candidly, filtering emotional responses so that we remain focused on the common good. For me, one of the most inspiring examples of grit was demonstrated by Naohiro Masuda, the superintendent of the Fukushima Daini plant that survived the Tōhoko earthquake and tsunami in 2011.

In their *HBR* article "How the Other Fukushima Plant Survived," Ranjay Gulati, Charles Casto, and Charlotte Krontiris describe how Masuda created psychological safety and commitment even though his team "felt the earthquake through the soles of their feet as they watched the sea heave sharks and cars across the plant's pavement." Their review of his leadership in an unimaginable crisis reveals how calmness and honesty fueled grit: "So he offered data, giving the workers an opportunity to confront and process the uncertainty for themselves. He prompted them to do their own sense-making: to reflect on how their emerging reality fit their assessment of risk . . . Because Masuda had so calmly presented his people with the uncertainty of their situation . . . they could embrace the unpredictable nature of their work." Masuda didn't tell people what to think or feel. He let his own actions and emotional state communicate psychological safety.

Masuda was able to mobilize vast amounts of relational potential in the days after a seventeen-meter wave, twelve meters higher than the facility was designed to survive, overwhelmed efforts to complete a controlled cooldown of the reactors. With no power, his plant was headed for an explosion and a meltdown. However, his teams managed to reconnect the most vulnerable reactor, Unit 1, to power, a superhuman effort by any standards: "The cables came in 200-meter sections that weighed a ton each. Daini workers would have to lay more than nine kilometers' worth to hook up the three disabled units . . . they would have about 24 hours to complete the task. Under normal circumstances, a job like that would take twenty people using heavy machinery more than a month to finish." They had no heavy machinery. Every section required two hundred people to lift and shift it manually into place with the risk of radioactive fallout ever present in their minds.

The sister plant, Fukushima Daiiachi, may have had a very different experience had it had its own Masuda.

When people experience psychological safety resulting from grit, they have more energy available to get things done. They stop worrying about themselves and focus on doing what needs to be done. In this sense, psychological safety is more emotional than rational.

Leaders who maintain focus and avoid distraction have a presence that impacts not only how they're perceived by others but also their teams' productivity, performance, and collaboration. They have better relationships, which correlates strongly with psychological safety.

Go High guidance

· Stay calm under pressure.
· Show up with a positive attitude and energy.
· Recover quickly from setbacks and disappointment.
· Take the blame, don't spread it.
· Show more grit than growl.

6

Lift Others Up

How can we help people to learn and change when humans are programmed to avoid taking risks or looking incompetent?

Overview

People who worked with the Hollywood actor Jack Lemmon during the latter stages of his career would hear him speak of his desire "to send the elevator back down." Lemmon was keen to smooth the way for others, encouraging, guiding, and supporting them where he could. He wanted to Lift Others Up, helping them realize their dreams. He recognized his own status and position, and wanted to use them to benefit other people, particularly those just starting out in the industry.

From a leadership perspective, Lift Others Up centers on our ability to coach, mentor, and teach others. As Harvard professor of business Rosabeth Moss Kanter observed, lifting others up is about recognizing people's value and effort, apportioning credit where it's due, celebrating success, and giving back. When we share our own knowledge and experience and identify and nurture potential in colleagues, we can inspire them to learn, grow, and achieve greatness.

As a graduate student, I chose to study the psychology of learning other languages. The subject resonated with me at the time: I was struggling with learning Danish well enough to survive graduate studies at a Danish university. (They didn't speak Australian, funnily enough.) One of the most important insights I gained was that our battle to learn new things and develop as adults is primarily a social one. Our brains don't lose the ability to learn, but we feel there's too much at stake socially and in terms of ego and pride to take a chance on stretching ourselves.

This insight has had a profound impact on how I approach coaching, teaching, and organizational transformation. Leaders must address people's fear of looking stupid by providing relational support to help a learner overcome their inner skeptic, judge, and punisher. If you don't, learners will become increasingly resistant, frightened of reliving the experience of being consciously incompetent.

All change requires learning new things and then not letting old practices creep back into our habits. We have to learn to work with new people and new bosses. We have to go to work in a new way, or not at all. Lift Others Up is at the heart of growth mindset in terms of helping others grow. Understanding what it takes to learn makes leaders better coaches and teachers, which is highly correlated to effectiveness in the Growth Mindset Leadership 360 assessment.

Benefits
· Facilitates more successful learning and change.
· Builds confidence to tackle new challenges and relationships.

· Creates higher levels of operational quality and safety.
· Reduces self-interest and isolation.

Rise

In 2019, the Springboks, South Africa's rugby union team, braced themselves for yet another against-the-odds finals appearance in Japan. On November 2 in Yokohama, their head coach, Rassie Erasmus, gave a rallying speech to the team members about their individual stories, their brotherhood, and their opportunity to inspire a nation back home. The team's captain, Siya Kolisi, was keenly affected by the kaleidoscopic effects of being lifted up personally, as a squad, and as a nation. On the eve of the final, he and his wife, Rachel, compiled lists of all the things they wanted to do to help their country if the team won the Cup.

Kolisi entered the world on the last day of the apartheid regime: June 16, 1991. During his childhood, he endured both hardship and privilege. His life mirrored the peaks and troughs of a country revived, one still coming to terms with the injustices and inequalities of its recent past. When Kolisi was born, his parents were both teenagers, unable to look after a baby. He grew up mostly under the care of his maternal grandmother in the Zwide township near Port Elizabeth. Violent escapades, alcohol, and substance abuse were all part of his early years.

However, the youthful promise he showed on the rugby pitch opened doors for Kolisi. First, he was offered scholarships at the highly regarded Grey Junior and Grey High schools in Port Elizabeth. Later, on leaving school, his dedication, effort, and talent were rewarded with an offer of a professional career in rugby, which would have been almost unthinkable under apartheid.

In 1995, days after Kolisi's fourth birthday, the Springboks won their first World Cup final. The team that took the field that day in Johannesburg was predominantly white. Twenty-four years later, Kolisi, the team's first Black captain, raised the World Cup trophy in the air in victory alongside his multi-ethnic team. The imagery showed that the sport and the nation had traveled a long way.

Kolisi's autobiography, *Rise*, was published in 2021, two years after South Africa's successful World Cup campaign and victory over England in the final. The book's title is a description of Kolisi's own life experiences but also an exhortation to others. "The title refers to my journey from a township childhood to captain of a World Cup-winning Springbok team," Kolisi explains in an author's note, "and also to the progress that I am working to bring about in my beloved South Africa. Most of all, however, 'rise' is the English meaning of my mother's name Phakama." The title reminds me of Maya Angelou's poem "Still I Rise," which depicts her determination to thrive in the face of discrimination against people of color in the USA.

> You may write me down in history
> With your bitter, twisted lies,
> You may trod me in the very dirt
> But still, like dust, I'll rise.

Kolisi is the first to recognize that there remains much to do to address social injustices and abuses in his homeland. Like Lemmon before him, Kolisi has sought to use his own status and influence to help Lift Others Up. In April 2020, he and his wife launched The Kolisi Foundation. It's intended to assist disadvantaged communities hit hardest by the COVID-19 pandemic and to address systemic inequalities in South Africa, such as gender-based violence, food insecurity, and unequal access to education and sport. As they state on the Foundation's website, the couple "are compelled by a strong conviction that every small act of change matters." When we lift one person up, we create the potential for another to follow, in a perpetual domino effect.

Encouragement

How do we as leaders encourage others? One way is to listen intently to what staff have to say. We can invite their opinion and factor their varied, occasionally conflicting, perspectives into our decisions. Another way is to amplify what they say and do, extending their reach and impact. We need to find ways to enable others to take risks, to challenge and question us when they disagree, to lift them up when they struggle or when things go wrong. We need to be available to provide feedback as they exercise their curiosity and explore.

What goes around comes around, as my grandma used to say. Our role as leaders is to create a positive circle of influence and encouragement. Sometimes we seek the input of a brains trust, as happens at Pixar. On other occasions we're members of that brains trust, and it's down to us to guide, advise, and provide constructive criticism to help others to develop and grow. In all these different ways, we can demonstrate care for and interest in those we lead, facilitating safe learning spaces and cultures. Through our encouragement, we can establish what the humanistic psychologist Carl Rogers called the *freedom to learn*.

While purpose and mastery can catalyze a desire to learn and unlearn, human development is profoundly enhanced by relationships. Conversely, isolation and disconnection slow learning or send it into reverse. We may love e-learning, YouTube, and TikTok, but there's no substitute for caring teachers, colleagues, leaders, and coaches when it comes to putting learning into practice. Learning at work will remain a highly complex process of trial and failure. Of confidence-denting experiences and social moments of truth. When we receive encouragement, we learn and grow. At least, that's what I see in my work and research. Leaders who teach, encourage, and support their people create learning, productivity, and growth.

But we learn at work even without encouragement. Humans are sponges. When we lack encouragement or face toxicity, we don't stop learning. We learn to cope or survive, to un-grow. We learn to protect ourselves and to remain in our comfort zone.

The point of encouragement is that it directs learning toward growth and helps us deal with the discomfort of passing through the consciously incompetent phase of any development process. We can learn to grow, but only if we learn together.

Even the smallest acts of kindness and encouragement can have a ripple effect on individual team members or entire organizations. Genuine engagement and recognition make people feel seen, heard, and valued. This was how the South African rugby players were made to feel before the World Cup final. When they stepped onto the field, they were lifted up by each other, their supporters, and a higher purpose. England was quite simply blown away.

Lift Others Up guidance
· Recognize and value others' efforts and achievements.
· Teach and coach, sharing your know-how and experience.
· Show strong interest in others' perspectives and ideas.
· Encourage others to learn and take reasonable risks.
· Never underestimate a team with a strong purpose.

7

Team Up

How can we achieve alignment within and between teams, fostering supportive relationships that are about safety and respect rather than status and privilege?

Overview

Team Up is about how we create emotional engagement and develop social sensitivity. It's not only about respect. It's also about managing the emotions of an unhappy customer or having the skills to resolve a conflict at work. It's about feeling safe enough to speak up. It's about bridging gaps in experience, knowledge, and background to find common ground and new ideas.

When we Team Up, we can access team intelligence and mobilize energy and enthusiasm. In a world dependent on collective know-how, critical thinking, and team effort, leaders lacking Team Up are reducing creativity, getting stuck in biases, and stifling team intelligence. When we Team Up, we know more, and what we know is more useful.

Team Up allows us to span boundaries and create hot spots so that everyone benefits from the collective expertise, experience, know-how, technical proficiency, and creativity. It's essential in the modern workplace, where everyone is different and looking to be included, and where we need all the human potential we can muster to solve the challenges of the four ages. With Team Up, we can celebrate our authentic selves, uniqueness, and strengths, and we can add to and draw from our community. Team Up is founded on inclusion and the integration of multiple skills and perspectives and invites diversity. It defies any move toward uniformity, homogeneity, groupthink, or protective peer pressure.

In our VUCAH world, most leaders struggle to address complex, interacting issues alone, whether it's as individuals, single organizations, or solitary nations. Deep expertise in a single field can be helpful, but only in combination with other areas of practice and inquiry. Constructive challenging and interdisciplinarity can lead to more innovative products, services, and practices. Our similarities can serve to connect us, but when our differences are harnessed via a common purpose and Team Up, we can propel ourselves forward.

Collaboration is the recurring theme for success in the four ages. However, we'll have to Team Up in ways that defy human genetic preferences for stable groups and relationships. Fast teaming and nimble networks are how we'll drive innovation and accelerate change in the future.

Kanter's research on leading positive change reveals that when we partner with others, creativity and performance improve significantly, which noticeably affects organizational culture. To Team Up effectively, then, we must seek out and connect—online or in person—with new people and ideas both within and outside our teams, organizations, and communities.

If we want to learn and grow, we must challenge our biases, stereotypes, preconceptions, and assumptions by actively seeking out alternative perspectives, listening intently, and trying to understand what others do, how they do it, and why.

Benefits
· Creates psychological safety.
· Increases information sharing and improves quality.
· Includes people with different experiences and cultures.
· Drives innovation and fast change.

Collaboration
Nothing brings the need for collective action more clearly into focus than crises that disregard the borders and boundaries of personhood, business, and nation. Financial collapses, climate catastrophes, and disease have punctuated the first three decades of the twenty-first century, challenging our infrastructures and global institutions and highlighting the need for new knowledge, capabilities, organization methods, and most of all, partnerships.

The COVID-19 pandemic catalyzed numerous new collaborations within and across the health sector and scientific research communities. Public organizations and private enterprises came together. Former competitors became partners. All were motivated by shared causes: containment, prevention, and survival. As Jesse Bump, Peter Friberg, and David Harper note in a *British Medical Journal* article written at the height of the pandemic, "The imperative of finding collaborative and collective solutions—solidarity—has never been more obvious, or more urgent."

Scientists in China and Australia, for example, successfully mapped the virus genome in January 2020, making their findings freely available. Over the next five months, the genome was sequenced over three thousand times as researchers expanded the knowledge base about the original virus and its mutations, facilitating the development of effective vaccines. Meanwhile, disparate health-care organizations cohered into health systems, with frontline staff dealing with COVID-19 patients supported by other personnel, irrespective of their specialisms.

In *Orbiting the Giant Hairball*, Gordon MacKenzie explores how relationships impact innovation and creativity. His unusual book title reflects the challenge many creative people face when at work. Orbit too close to the hairball, you'll get stuck in conformity and compliance. Shoot too high and far from the hairball, you'll fly off into deep space with all the other undiplomatic rebels. MacKenzie argues that we need to find a comfortable orbit that's close enough to have an impact and benefit from corporate resources, but not so close that we risk losing our individuality in brain-numbing loyalty. (The Goldilocks spot, if you like.)

The need to balance independence, dependence, and interdependence is expressed by the term *Diplomatic Rebels*, which came out of Lego's Future Lab. For budding "intrapreneurs"—people who want to bring about meaningful change in larger organizations—the Diplomatic Rebels have some inspiring principles that contribute well to an understanding of what growth mindset looks like in the context of innovation:

1. Accept other people will hate your project.
2. Only break rules you understand.
3. Build a tribe.
4. Write love letters.
5. Make people shine.

Four of the five principles are aimed specifically at building "nimble networks," a phrase Morten Hansen, a management professor at the University of California, uses in *Collaboration: How Leaders Avoid the Traps, Create Unity, and Reap Big Results* to describe small, agile teams that can quickly adapt to changing circumstances and achieve their goals through collaboration.

The point is that Teaming Up is good for creativity as long as you don't create groupthink or exclude important ideas and people from the outside. It's the right balance of me and we. It's about interdependence and mutual respect.

Teaming

In many of the examples of collaboration I've given, success has depended on quickly building relationships across professional, cultural, and identity boundaries. Teamwork is no longer a slow process of getting to know colleagues over years. It's now about teaming—creating a fast and less permanent relationship that involves weak ties, candor, swift trust, radical inclusion, and physical and virtual interactions, and enables learning. It's about collaborating with people you know as well as people you don't know yet.

In *Teaming: How Organizations Learn, Innovate, and Compete in the Knowledge Economy*, Amy Edmondson argues that in today's knowledge economy, no one person or team can possess all the knowledge and expertise necessary to solve complex problems. Instead, she says, teams must be able to come together quickly and efficiently, drawing on diverse perspectives and knowledge to solve problems and innovate. She redefines teamwork as "teaming" to reflect a paradigm shift from teamwork oriented to execution of plans, to teamwork for learning and innovation. "Teaming is a verb. It is a dynamic activity, not a bounded, static entity. It is largely determined by the mindset and practices of teamwork, not by the design and structures of effective teams. Teaming is teamwork on the fly. It involves coordinating and collaborating without the benefit of stable team structures, because many operations, such as hospitals, power plants, and military installations, require a level of staffing flexibility that makes stable team composition rare."

Some of the biggest barriers to teaming are connected to diversity. We struggle to make quick connections with people who come from very different professional backgrounds. Due to specialization, occupational cultures have become some of the biggest cultural barriers to teaming along with ethnic and generational differences.

The design of common organizational goals is often intended to break down barriers and encourage cross-functional collaboration. However, without emotional involvement, this is almost impossible. Leaders must hone their empathy skills and help develop empathy in teams so that teams can successfully connect, challenge, learn, resolve, and act. This includes encouraging healthy disagreement and solving interpersonal, occupational, and organizational conflicts. Boundary spanning isn't always easy. As Edmondson argues, teaming in a diverse workplace requires a collaborative mindset. We have to care enough about our purpose and each other to deal with the uncertainty of working with people with whom we share little prior experience.

When we Team Up, we must move beyond traditional hierarchies of knowledge or status into what Edmondson describes as a "reciprocal interdependence, where back-and-forth communication and coordination are essential to getting the work done." If we aren't asking for help ourselves, we must be ready to provide it, to listen, to share knowledge, to explain, and to help somebody else make a breakthrough.

When most people prefer relationships where they're in charge (controlling), disconnected (cynical), or following (complying), Team Up offers an uncomfortable vision of collaborating with a growth mindset. Our DNA and cultural programming may mean teaming doesn't come naturally. But if we overcome these barriers, we can realize our full relational potential.

Team Up guidance

· Make it easy for people to get to know you.
· Listen for the unsaid—what's hidden is often more important than what's said.
· Foster emotional involvement within and between teams across the organization.
· Help others in significant ways.
· Bump into strangers—and strike up random conversations.

8

Summary

In what way is growth mindset a paradigm shift?

The six Safe2Great growth principles present the framework for a paradigm shift in leadership from control to commitment. Commitment-based leadership can better meet the needs of the twenty-first century, where technological, social, and environmental change inspire and scare in equal measure. When people are committed, they change faster, collaborate better, and innovate more profoundly. That's the commitment premium.

Commitment in the four ages needs to be driven by a purpose that binds not only the efforts and ideas of the members of your organization, but also the efforts and ideas of all the external members of your ecosystem. Dolphins Transform.

People need effective pathways to achieve their dreams and visions that engage and promote mastery. Dolphins Aim High.

Creative and critical thinking, the newsmart, requires a new level of humility, curiosity, and playfulness. Dolphins Explore.

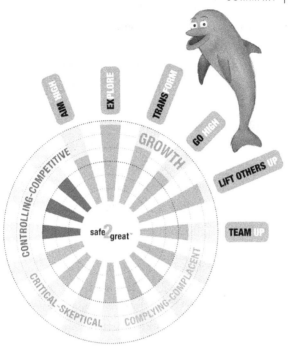

Emotional engagement, positivity, and grit help us recover from backslides, disappointments, and dead-ends and build confidence. Dolphins Go High.

We all must unlearn and learn new things, and we learn best through small successes and the support of caring colleagues and bosses. Dolphins Lift Others Up.

Collaboration is one of our human superpowers that helps us be smarter, more innovative, and more humane. Dolphins Team Up.

Leading with a growth mindset is not about excelling at only one of these six principles. They're profoundly interlinked. Each one relies in part on some or all of the others to become fully realized. To Explore is enhanced by Team Up. To Lift Others Up is enhanced by Going High. To Aim High is enhanced by Transform. Balance between challenge and support drives the best outcomes like psychological safety and team performance. Together, these principles form a new psychology of leadership. While my research shows they exist less commonly in practice, they lead very commonly to high commitment.

My colleagues and I have asked thousands of people to describe a workplace culture that would be ideal for success in their respective industries, and they invariably describe these six principles, allowing for minor variations across professions and localities. This raises important questions: If most people want to work in organizations that adhere to the growth principles, why are they strongly in evidence in only 30% of the organizations we've surveyed? Why is it still considered unusual, even quirky, to lead with a growth mindset?

In Part II, The Dark Side, I present some possible answers to these questions. I highlight why the protective mindset continues to dominate our relationships, teams, and organizations, making it difficult to implement the six growth principles.

Many organizations throughout the world have identified growth mindset as an area of strategic focus. However, they're now encountering the difficulties that invariably emerge between aspiration and application. Implementing growth mindset is not a new go2market strategy, new CRM system, or major reorganization. It requires leaders to grow and to create a reinforcing organizational culture that supports growth. But when many leaders and corporate cultures exhibit controlling leadership and protective mindsets, the Safe2Great concepts take time to seed and take root. Many leaders are happy the way things are. I hope this book goes some way toward changing that attitude.

What does controlling leadership look like? Well, I think it looks like a bloat of hippos.

PART II

The Dark Side

Why are the growth mindset principles uncommon in teams and organizations?

What prevents growth?

What are the behaviors and effects associated with a protective mindset?

Why is work an unfair playing field favoring controlling leaders?

What are the costs of protecting the status quo?

9

Why Leaders Choose Control Rather than Commitment

What drives leaders to prefer the thrill and safety of control rather than the benefits of commitment?

Organizations are neither safe nor fair

I've long been fascinated by and appalled at the examples throughout history of clever people, ordinary people, people who should have known better making terrible mistakes or treating other humans with systematic cruelty and our planet with breathtaking neglect. I ask myself how a human could make sense of their job and lack the ethical, professional, and moral compass to somehow say "stop." Examples that come to mind are camp guards in Nazi Germany, energy traders working for Enron, and the managers who sent the shuttle *Challenger* into space. These people operated within organizations where poor, sometimes abhorrent, outcomes were acceptable and normal—desirable, even. In some of these cases, the outcomes were the result of an organization, and the people working in it, becoming stuck. Stuck in the sense that their culture or mindset made change and growth impossible. They had become obsessed with managing internal rivalries between powerful bosses, ambitious colleagues, and overconfident experts rather than considering the external impact of their work. Politics had overwhelmed or killed their original purpose. They were stuck in a protective mindset.

Three of the most influential forces that can cause people to develop ways of working that lead to bad outcomes are controlling leadership, peer pressure, and psychological withdrawal. These forces stem from a combination of our genetic makeup and our cultural traditions, and they're at the core of the dark side of leadership. I'll explore all three forces and how the Safe2Great model helps us understand and tackle them before they create less than stellar outcomes. These forces aren't unique to certain types of organizations or cultures; they're ubiquitous. We might say that they lie buried in every human like a primordial rogue virus ready to be activated under the "right" influences and circumstances.

In this sense, I need to dispel a myth about human behavior that prevents us from seeing the impact of leadership, culture, and group pressure on human behavior. We've been trained to think that human behavior is based on free will and autonomy and that we make decisions actively, responsibly, and rationally. While this view of human behavior is compelling and central to how we attribute guilt in our legal and moral systems, it muddies the role that leaders, culture, and colleagues play in shaping our behavior. In Part I, I wrote that because commitment is a choice, its biggest enemy is control, but often we give up our right to choose in return for the protection of strong bosses, traditional cultures, and powerful peers. Most of the time, we aren't aware of this happening. This is one of the cognitive biases that keeps us operating with protective mindsets.

Fire

On November 19, 1987, the day after the horrific fire at one of London's busiest Underground stations, King's Cross, a young music teacher recovering from burns spoke to a journalist from the *Times* newspaper, asking: "Why did they send me straight into the fire? I could see them burning. I could hear them screaming. Why didn't someone take charge?" One hundred commuters were injured and thirty-one died that day.

The fire started when a commuter riding a wooden escalator carelessly dropped a glowing match, which landed in garbage lying underneath the steps. A lack of training, inadequate preventive maintenance, and an inability to think and act adaptively under pressure allowed the small escalator fire to become a "flashover" within fifteen minutes. A jet of high-temperature flame burst into the ticketing hall, killing or burning everyone who hadn't been evacuated. The cooked flesh of some of the survivors was literally peeling off their bones.

Some of what transpired was unimaginable at the time, so we should bear in mind the historical context before we criticize the actions of anyone who was caught up in the disaster. We can, though, use the case to explore the impact of a protective-minded leadership on how people respond in emergencies. The King's Cross fire has served as a lesson in how to prepare for and prevent disasters in many industries since. In fact, the lessons learned have probably saved countless lives.

A public inquiry into the incident revealed that a range of managerial and operational deficiencies—including the haphazard implementation of a ban on smoking on the Underground which had been introduced in 1984—contributed to the London Underground's and the London Fire Brigade's ineffective response. For the purposes of this book, the story demonstrates how job roles, leadership (or lack thereof), and a culture of complacency created a situation where people didn't act according to common sense but with reckless disregard for safety. The problem that day wasn't that someone failed to respond to the smoke or the flames in the escalator when they were insignificant enough to be extinguished quickly; it was how controlling leaders rendered their employees so incapable, so thoughtless, and so powerless in the face of impending disaster. Too many people didn't think or act very effectively that day. Too many people didn't have the right keys or know how to use the fire equipment. Too many trains passed through the station without stopping. People failed that day because the organization prevented them from succeeding.

The managers of the London Underground in the late 1980s weren't complacent. They were bureaucratic and territorial, controlling and monitoring staff behaviors and maintaining extremely tight silos. As Charles Duhigg writes in *The Power of Habit*, many unwritten rules of the Underground contributed to the disaster. One of those rules was "The fire department should never be contacted unless absolutely necessary." This rule may seem utterly counterintuitive, but it's indicative of how excessive control distorts and confounds common sense.

The key point I'd like to emphasize through the King's Cross case is that incompetent, uncooperative, unproductive work is primarily driven by poor leadership and a dysfunctional culture rather than incompetent employees. When performance is poor, we need to improve the quality of leadership, not criticize staff's lack of talent, proactivity, or ambition. Duhigg observes that organizations aren't the collaborative, constructive communities that we dream of working for: "Rather most workplaces are made up of fiefdoms where executives compete for power and credit, often in hidden skirmishes that make their own performances appear superior and their rivals' seem worse. Divisions compete for resources and sabotage each other to steal glory. Bosses pit their subordinates against one another so that no one can mount a coup. Companies aren't families. They're battlefields in a civil war."

The description of workplaces as "battlefields in a civil war" illustrates what I mean by the dark side of leadership and organizations. It's the us vs. them, winner takes all, survival of the fittest version of the organizational world. The London Underground fire demonstrates how leadership and culture are based not on effectiveness, what's best for the customer, or a noble purpose, but on politics, personal success, and ego.

To implement a growth mindset and create a great organization, we need to understand that much of what we're doing today as leaders doesn't make people feel safe. I call it *controlling leadership*, but the impact on others is a reduction in psychological safety—it makes others compete (fight), shut up (flight), or keep to themselves (freeze).

The dark side of leadership is embodied by the Hippo, Snail, and Clam. But before we meet them, let's look at *diminishers*.

Diminishers

Controlling leaders dull our intelligence.

In *Multipliers*, Liz Wiseman argues that organizations aren't full of multipliers like Tom Brady, but rather *diminishers*, who consider themselves indispensable to their organizations.

They're Satya Nadella's know-it-alls, confident of their own knowledge and experience, and distrustful and disrespectful of what others have to offer. Diminishers undermine their teams, centralize control, hoard knowledge, and micromanage. They're self-centered and self-promoting, quick to claim credit for successes and to point the finger of blame when things don't go well. They make others feel less intelligent and less confident.

The ability of diminishers to progress to the most senior levels of organizations is an important—and often ignored—uncomfortable truth of organizational life and politics. The fact is, as I noted earlier, organizations aren't always fair, and they don't operate as level playing fields.

Diminishers, particularly those who lean toward authoritarianism, often seek to distort reality to cultivate their own mythology. They leverage the misguided loyalty of their faithful followers, peddling untruths that are accepted and reinforced through repetition. This explains why senior Boeing executives can blame foreign pilots rather than their own design flaws for fatal accidents, former US President Donald Trump can convince millions that an election was stolen from him, and Russian President Vladimir Putin can portray the invasion of a neighboring state as a "special military operation" to protect the Ukrainian people and de-Nazify their government.

Such leaders show contempt for anyone who doesn't share their convictions, hunting down, bullying, and shaming critics and whistleblowers. They quash dissent by taking advantage of the average person's dislike of conflict and fear of reprisals. They know how to use a lack of psychological safety and resulting conspiracy of silence for their own benefit. The cyclist Lance Armstrong offers a powerful example of how this works.

Professional cycling through much of the 1990s and early 2000s was thoroughly corrupt. During this period, the sport was renowned for doping practices, in particular the use of erythropoietin (EPO), which boosts red blood cell production and has a dramatic effect on a cyclist's speed, endurance, and climbing ability. The peloton's unofficial code of silence was policed by dominant figures, such as multiple Tour de France winner Lance Armstrong, who was later proven to have benefited personally and financially from the widespread cheating.

Even those who didn't dope were persuaded that it was in their best interests not to break ranks if they wished to continue earning their living from cycling. Signs of dissent were crushed by enforcers. During the 2004 Tour de France, for example, race leader Armstrong was caught on camera admonishing fellow cyclist Filippo Simioni, forcing him to return to the main peloton rather than remain in the day's breakaway group, signaling with a zipped-lip gesture that he should remain silent. Simioni's offense had been to testify against Dr. Michele Ferrari, Armstrong's trainer, in a sporting fraud trial in Italy.

It was later confirmed by the US Anti-Doping Agency's 2012 investigation not only that Ferrari was integral to Armstrong's own doping program but also that Armstrong's bullying wasn't confined to members of other teams like Simioni. In addition, there was evidence of threatening behavior in Armstrong's interactions with former teammates, whom he suspected might betray his secrets, and journalists who doubted the probity of his success. Control was paramount, and fear was the tool he used to achieve it. Armstrong was a Hippo.

Metaphors for change

In Part I, I introduced the Dolphin to reflect the dynamism, agility, smartness, and curiosity associated with a growth mindset. I now want to introduce three more metaphors from the natural world to explain more about the dark side: the Hippo, the Snail, and the Clam. Hippos control, self-promote, and cajole others into following; Snails conform, self-protect, and cope; and Clams criticize, are self-righteous, and resist.

These metaphors are intentionally simple and humorous. I've found that they resonate with both audiences and the people I coach, conveying tough messages in a manner that's both palatable and memorable. No one likes being told that the way they lead or behave is problematic. A touch of humor can help create a connection, enabling the real work to begin. They're usually self-designated and not imposed by others, especially others higher up the corporate hierarchy. They should never be used to belittle, exclude, or dominate.

I chose the Hippo not only because of its reputation as the most dangerous animal in Africa, but also because of the way it breaks wind and defecates. A hippo fart is memorable for its volume, and when a hippo defecates it spins its tail and spreads excrement in every direction. Hippos also are renowned for their fierce territoriality and their preference for living in mud pools. Lack of transparency is crucial to their effectiveness. Hippos love mud.

Snails have an endearing softness to them. They lack real backbone and retreat into their shells when threatened. They hesitate, preferring to wait and see rather than stick their necks out too far. Snails represent excessive friendliness, captured by the sticky trail they leave behind them as they go. By conforming to rules, Snails avoid too much uncomfortable attention. A Snail's best defense is to go unnoticed.

Clams are fiercely independent. They are skeptical about others, prefer to live and work alone, and have a hard outer shell that protects them, especially if they shut their mouths. I've often heard people identifying themselves with the Clam, referencing the pearl that forms inside their shells. But keep in mind that it takes a lot of irritation to help that pearl form.

I use these metaphors to help people consider how their behaviors impact others. It's the Hippo's excrement, toxicity, and aggression that prevent others from growing, provoking their disengagement and demotivation. It's the Snail's sticky trail that binds us to the status quo. It's the closedness and antisocial qualities of the Clam that undermine our confidence and hope. And at the other end of the spectrum, it's the sharpness of the Dolphin's teeth that reminds us that growth can be challenging and uncomfortable at times.

When using the metaphors, there are two important things to keep in mind. First, when I say a leader is a Dolphin, Hippo, Snail, or Clam, I'm describing their current operating mode, not a personality trait. Mindset is both situational and stable over time and space. Second, there's good in all the mindsets. Hippos are setting direction and creating urgency. Snails are keeping people happy and collaborating. Clams are thinking independently and creatively. The negative effects aren't always intentional. They often spring from how they're doing things, or what they aren't doing.

I've chosen to give special attention to the Hippo because controlling leadership has a unique status in and impact on an organization's culture and its members' well-being. Controlling leadership really is the preferred or "go-to" approach in business. People who have a Hippo mindset are more likely to be promoted, more often solicited by senior leadership for ideas, and more likely to receive funding for projects. They benefit from the uneven playing field in organizations which this book is partially designed to challenge and disrupt.

If we want a growth culture, we must create a No Hippo Zone. But more on that later.

10

The Hippo

What happens when competition and control are the dominant leadership characteristics that shape organizational culture?

Overview

Robert Sutton is a professor of management science at Stanford University and has spent considerable time researching and writing about poor leadership and its detrimental effects. He published three books on the subject between 2007 and 2017: *The No Asshole Rule, Good Boss, Bad Boss*, and *The Asshole Survival Guide*. Sutton's "asshole" was the inspiration for my Hippo. Assholes at work are competitive, controlling, and self-promoting leaders and colleagues who perceive themselves to be special and above the pack. (At the time, I was unaware of Patrick Lencioni's term "highest paid person's opinion" (Hippo) and how he used it in his 2004 book *Death by Meeting*.)

Leaders operating with a Hippo mindset act in ways that make others feel undervalued, insulted, threatened, and uncomfortable. They're hostile, rivalrous, grandiose, self-obsessed, and undermining not only at work but also in their general interactions with other people.

In *The No Asshole Rule*, Sutton explains that organizations often prefer assholes because they can achieve short-term gains through their aggressive and disruptive behavior. The belief that assholes are "high performers" and their abrasive behavior "gets results" often leads companies to overlook their negative impact on the work environment. However, Sutton argues that any gains are often short-lived and outweighed by the negative impact of toxic behavior on employees' morale, productivity, and well-being. He says that a work environment that tolerates asshole leaders can lead to reduced morale, high turnover, and a lack of accountability, which can harm an organization's reputation and bottom line.

Asshole leaders bring out the worst in others, destroying opportunities for collaborative work, problem-solving, and innovation. They protect what they have, and they want more of it. Hippos foment conflict, anxiety, competition, resistance, compliance, and complacency. They force others to copy their excrement-throwing behaviors or to cope with or resist them by becoming Snail- or Clam-like. In this sense, Hippos make it hard for others to be themselves and realize their full potential.

Like the animal, Hippo leaders create fear, and the habitats in which they wallow are filled with tension and distrust. The people around them are often directly or indirectly persuaded to imitate their aggressive and controlling methods as a means of either survival or progression. To be recognized and promoted under a Hippo's leadership, it may be necessary to act like the Hippo—but without threatening their dominance. People begin to fight fire with fire, exacerbating an already combative environment.

Hippo traits

- Set unrealistic goals.
- Dismiss concerns or needs.
- Fight against sharing control.
- Dominate relationships.
- Punish people who don't deliver.
- Don't follow the rules.
- Draw attention to themselves.
- Show aggression and hostility.

Anger

Rashid sat quietly in his large corner office, sipping coffee while he read the morning newspapers. This was a daily ritual that accompanied his early arrival at the global headquarters of the manufacturing company where he was CEO. Today, though, was a little different. The previous evening, Rashid had been warned by the Chief of Investor Relations that an embarrassing story about the company would be on the front page of the business daily. Within the hour, he had to facilitate a summit on the organization's future involving executives from around the world.

During an uneasy night, Rashid had recalled months of frustration and anger over the failure of the company's new flagship product. It had cost him so much, including the chance of heading into early retirement at the height of his career. He'd had to struggle to regain the confidence of the board, promising not to go anywhere until things were fixed. He'd also made it clear that only he could solve the problem.

His blood boiled as he scanned the article. He felt the sting of old wounds as he read about how his organization had spent over $50 million to solve production problems. In reality, the damage to customer confidence and the boost to their industry rivals had cost far more than that. Meanwhile, his fifteen-year perfect record as CEO was now tarnished.

He tossed the speech prepared by the Chief of Communications on the floor. Rashid was going to give the gathered executives a piece of his mind. He needed people to know he was going nowhere and that if they didn't shape up, they'd be out. When he entered the conference room, he ignored everyone, marched to the lectern, checked his watch, slammed a copy of the newspaper down, and then let loose.

Broad-shouldered and tall, he paced up and down, scanning the room as if looking for someone to take the blame. It was one of the strongest collective reprimands I have witnessed in my career, humiliating for everyone in the room, terrible to watch, inaccurate, and completely unfair. It was an appalling, one-sided, and self-righteous tirade.

Those who had been closest to the project, in supply chain and product development, were angry and embarrassed. Some were ready to leave the company there and then. Sylvester, the project manager of the team tasked with fixing the problem, spoke up. He took a diplomatic approach as he attempted to defuse the situation, acknowledging that they should have done better but appealing for Rashid's guidance to help them get back on track. His efforts were greeted with sarcasm.

But for all the vitriol and anger, Rashid played it safe that day, taking the easy way out. He did what he needed to do to protect himself, to stay in control, to be superior and independent. He performed the role of an authoritarian and coercive leader. He blamed and accused others, displaying inappropriate aggression and disrespect, ignoring his own complicity, and patronizing the other executives. Yet all he managed to do was project his own frustration and fear onto other people, effectively outsourcing his emotions.

From Rashid's perspective, he was modeling true leadership, convinced that by taking a tough stance he was being courageous and meeting the board's expectations. He couldn't see that he was staying within his own comfort zone and instilling an organizational culture of blame, denial, procrastination, and sabotage, where people who felt disrespected might actively seek to damage the company. He failed to seize the moment and play for great. He missed an opportunity for growth.

While displays of anger may briefly command people's attention, what those people really remember is how they were made to feel rather than the words they heard or the arguments made. Anger tends to confuse people rather than focus their attention. This is because it generates fear. As Amy Edmondson notes in *The Fearless Organization*: "Fear inhibits learning. Research in neuroscience shows that fear consumes physiologic resources, diverting them from parts of the brain that manage working memory and process new information. This impairs analytic thinking, creative insight, and problem solving."

When people feel bad, when they believe that they've been treated unfairly, they don't respond well. If you direct your anger at a colleague, they're unlikely to increase their commitment. Instead, they're likely to feel resentment, self-doubt, and distrust. At best, they may try to prove you wrong. At worst, they may leave the organization. Beyond the fight-or-flight instinct, fear doesn't motivate. It has no place in a complex, knowledge-based, and collaborative workplace.

The blame game

When Rashid treated people disrespectfully and apportioned blame, he created unnecessary friction within the company. The months that followed were filled with recrimination. Many good people left, and others became disengaged. Rashid failed to assess the impact of his own behavior on project meetings, which had made it almost impossible for the truth to be shared during the months and years leading up to the crisis.

If Rashid had practiced a growth mindset, entering his own discomfort zone, he could have accepted his own role in his organization's problems and apologized to those people whose advice he had ignored. With courage, he could have shown vulnerability and humility, asking his colleagues to help him rebuild the organization. Together, they could have fixed the problems, learned from their collective mistakes, and rethought how they worked together to avoid a similar issue in the future. Instead, he gave vent to his anger. He chose the path of protection over that of creation, leaving others to pick up the pieces. He reinforced the blame game rather than kick-start a healthy circle of accountability.

Authoritarian leaders like Rashid never take responsibility for the hidden costs of their controlling actions. They find other ways to explain or deal with the consequences of a callous and disrespectful leadership style. In our coaching sessions, Rashid continued to bemoan a lack of competence among the company's middle-managers and the paucity of talented people who could be relied on. He was blind to how his leadership impacted others and had contributed to a profound, systemic problem, an environment where it was too dangerous to speak candidly or challenge the CEO's opinions or decisions, even when he was clearly wrong.

The system continued to protect him, failing to reveal those hidden costs. It seemed that outside of our coaching interactions, Rashid was rarely challenged, rarely received feedback that contradicted his view of the world. His closest colleagues pandered to him, commenting on how much the organization needed his strength and wisdom, while the HR department neglected to correlate staff turnover with his leadership style, despite frequent mentions of it in exit interviews.

Other authoritarian leaders in the organization applauded his methods. His outburst had reassured them that their way of leading was the right way, a manifestation of their own authenticity. They didn't need to apologize for being unreasonable or coercive in the future. They didn't need to accept responsibility for their part in a problem. It was always someone else's fault, even when no scapegoat could be found. But not only did Rashid's approach to leadership remove any sense of psychological safety from his company, it also stopped people from speaking up about other issues. As a result, new product defects emerged within the year, making a bad problem even worse. (But that's another story.)

The pantomime of power

Rashid's story and the detrimental effects of his behavior are neither new nor unusual.

Why, then, does control remain the most common leadership model if we know how harmful it can be?

Because it works.

Whether you're Lance Armstrong, Donald Trump, or the head of the local school band, controlling leadership works because it offers the vision of success via control, stability, and power. These things are especially desired by organizations and people in times of uncertainty and danger. In many crucial moments, decisiveness and toughness are considered the most effective choice. It's partially due to the human obsession with heroes and unchecked hubris. Despite the warnings of philosophers like Homer, Plato, and Sophocles, we prefer vanity over humility, indulgence over self-control.

"Fear and wonder, a powerful combination," says Gracchus, a senator of Rome in Ridley Scott's 2000 movie *Gladiator*. Lance Armstrong's story illustrates how organizations and individual leaders both benefit when they conspire to create a culture based on control. It also reveals that controlling leaders and cultures like to conceal their detritus. They use stories, and sometimes facts, to feed the underlying belief that "the ends justify the means." That the trail to glory is marked by noble sacrifice and famous victories rather than ugly retrenchments, lies, coercion, bribery, and drug abuse. The pantomime of power involves leaders using symbols, gestures, or rituals to create the appearance of superiority, success, and worthiness. When you're above the fray, you can act with impunity. You can break ethical, legal, and social rules because you're special. Rule-breaking is a key attribute of Hippos. The remarkable fact is that we're so willing to ignore or accept our heroes' bad, unethical, and illegal behaviors. As Jeffrey Pfeffer writes in his controversial book *7 Rules of Power*, the last and most powerful rule is "Success excuses (almost) everything . . . Simply put, once you are on top, at least in some sense of that term, what you did to get there will be forgotten, forgiven, or possibly both."

Pfeffer isn't entirely sure why this is true, but he explores one potential culprit: cognitive dissonance theory, or humans' ability to think consistently in relation to beliefs and interpretations they have about the world and the people in it. In this case it translates as: If someone is successful, they probably have attributes that make them worthy of that success. Once we've anchored our mind on something being true or good, we ignore, downplay, or dispute any facts or evidence to the contrary. Our mind is wired in many ways for preserving or protecting existing ideas rather than growing new ones.

I was a huge fan of Armstrong. I believed he was the greatest athlete of his time. I fell for the story about his successful fight against cancer. He became an inspirational figure for me. He was determined and charismatic, a cancer survivor, and a world-class success. I was in awe. And in my magical state of awe and wonder, I wasn't interested in the swirling rumors or the critical facts or anomalies. I never considered that winning seven Tour de France titles is not only amazing but also extremely unlikely—impossible, even. His apparent defeat of logic, defiance of physical limitations, and almost supernatural ability were beguiling. A big part of me wanted it to be true no matter what. By branding himself as a cancer survivor, Armstrong was able to deflect attention from his performance and maintain the illusion of innocence—until, like so many heroes before him, he was betrayed by former allies.

Hippo leaders stay in power because they attract attention, know important people, are well funded, attract talent, and have enormous influence on real decisions. The fact that they also create toxic workplaces and unhappy societies is overlooked or ignored. Possibly the most controversial example of a Hippo is Jack Welch, whom David Gelles, a *New York Times* reporter, characterized as "The Man Who Broke Capitalism" in his book with the same title. One of the many uncomfortable truths the book revealed about Welch's success is that boards, bankers, investors, and even presidents prefer tough business leaders, ideally male ones. It also reveals that while Welch was and still is revered as a leader, he left GE on a pathway to financial disaster.

Welch was great at creating value for shareholders, but he created it by cutting the value creation capabilities of GE companies in the longer term. He made GE and its shareholders rich by growing on paper through offshoring manufacturing, outsourcing functions, and "buying rather than building." He was lucky to get out when he did, according to Gelles. GE was a hugely successful company when Welch took over in 1981. Welch left in 2001. In 2018, after 122 years in business, GE's spot on the Dow Jones Index was taken by a drugstore chain.

Gelles explains how Welch and other big bosses avoid responsibility: "In America, we worship our bosses . . . We put our chief executive up on pedestals, granting them wide latitude to influence our national discourse and endowing them with vast wealth while absolving them of accountability."

Paradoxically, controlling leaders generate the very consequences that justify their preferred leadership style. Rashid, for example, was the architect behind the conspiracy of silence at the heart of his company's failure, but by doubling down, blaming and punishing others, he exacerbated the situation. Leaders like Rashid are obsessed with rogue actors, disloyal team members, and rebels because they threaten their authority. In Rashid's ears, feedback and constructive criticism were a challenge to his authority and a sign of a lack of control. I tried to help him see these things as a healthy sign of commitment, but he found it easier to ignore me and the other people trying to help him.

Rashid's story neatly distills much of the research that has gone into this aspect of the Safe2Great model. When I encounter Hippos in my work, or in media coverage of high-profile businesses, I tend to find that their organizations are characterized by the privilege of the few, a lack of transparency, underground resistance, the deflection of accountability, and attempts to self-immunize against the consequences of either inevitable failure or the discovery of malpractice.

Re-reading stories of environmental and human disasters, ethical wrong turns, and illegal spending sprees, I'm reminded of how much we can learn from these examples about how leadership styles can affect how effectively, ethically, and inclusively organizations operate. I'm also inspired to continue fighting for a greater focus on building healthy cultures rather than an Enron-like obsession with hiring great talents and rank-and-yank performance reviews. The money showered on superstar performers would be far better spent on initiatives to improve leaders and teams everywhere. Everyone is capable of greatness if they're given a chance.

Controlling leadership that allows for no adaptation or deviation is nowhere near as effective as its advocates would like us to think. At GE—and at Boeing, as I'll discuss later—it impacted the performance, bottom line, and future viability of the organization and damaged internal and external relationships. The more unsafe the environment under a Hippo's leadership, the more people will become disengaged, demotivated, and uncommitted, seeking various methods either to resist or to protect themselves.

11

The Snail

What happens when leaders are complying and complacent, when friendliness and maintaining the status quo are the dominant leadership characteristics that shape organizational culture?

Overview

Essentially, Snails are likable people, warm and full of good intentions. But their protective strategies cause confusion and can incite contempt, complacency, and carelessness.

Overwhelmed in the face of big challenges, fearful of rejection, and reluctant to speak their minds, particularly to people more powerful than them, the Snail is hesitant, indecisive, and slow to act. Consensus under a Snail's leadership is not about inclusion, being heard, buy-in, or allocation of responsibilities. It's a directionless listening to all parties and over-reliance on authorities and bosses. For team members, it looks like indecision and treading too carefully, resulting in ineffectiveness. This, together with a reluctance to hold people to account, carries its own cost, as a Snail's colleagues and direct reports lose confidence in and respect for them, bypassing and excluding them in order to get things done.

The Snail's compliance is often described as *niceness*. But this is far from a compliment in workplaces where Hippos set a tone of dominance, rivalry, and independence. In those contexts, *nice* means weak, irrelevant, and incompetent. Nice suggests passivity, conformity, and a lack of adventure. Being nice almost always results in excluding important activities like inspiring others, pushing boundaries, and communicating boldly. Snails need to find a backbone instead of relying on a shell to hide. They need to provide firm direction, challenge constructively, and hold others to meeting their responsibilities.

Leaders operating with a Snail mindset are supportive and value relationships. They listen well and are quick to show gratitude and appreciation. They're cooperative, helpful, friendly, considerate, and loyal. But they can also be self-critical, needy, and overly sensitive to other people's emotions. They're often described by Hippos as gullible, lacking the ability to question and criticize when they know something isn't right, while quickly agreeing and conforming in their own quest for approval. They can lack a clear sense of personal authority, relying instead on rules and regulations to shape behaviors, which can make them seem excessively bureaucratic.

Snails lack both balance and determination; they're slow to adapt to shifting contexts and circumstances. Sometimes there's a need to be independent before being cooperative, to lead then follow, to challenge then conform. The Snail struggles with their instinct to offer sympathy when faced with difficult decisions, choosing the path of comfort and compliance rather than of growth. My Safe2Great research found that leaders with a Snail mindset don't foster psychological safety in their teams. Being nice doesn't equal creating safety. This finding can be explained by the fact that Snails don't always provide answers or make key decisions in a timely way. When they fail to put guardrails and core principles in place, their team members can lose whatever sense of safety they previously had.

Snail traits

· Worry excessively about outcomes.
· Are hesitant to make decisions or act.
· Seek more and more information.
· Believe that others know better.
· Want to wait and see what happens.
· Are concerned about rejection and being disliked.
· Fear making mistakes.
· Avoid criticism and disapproval.

Façade

Marek was always trying hard, putting on a brave face, smiling, taking the time to show he cared about his colleagues, regardless of their role. No birthday went by without a personal note or a little celebration. He was the chairman of the social club and oversaw the annual Christmas party. Marek knew people's names, where their spouses worked, how many children they had. People felt comfortable sharing their thoughts with him because he was a good listener, unselfish, and tolerant. Marek was experienced. He knew the customers, the products, and the way things worked.

From the outside, Marek looked happy, like a man who was comfortable in his work and his life. So it was a shock to everyone when he collapsed at work one day with a suspected stroke. In the middle of explaining how negotiations with the workers' union had run into unexpected difficulties, he looked up, wobbled on his chair, and slid to the floor. Everyone who saw it was shocked by the sight of their unconscious colleague being wheeled from the office on a gurney. None of them knew that Marek had been suffering for months from stomach pains and dizziness, and occasionally struggled to find his words.

Marek had led his insurance company's compensation and benefits team for ten years. But ever since a Hippo-like CEO had joined the company, he had found his working environment increasingly difficult and was struggling to cope. Summoned to the executive suite, Marek had been instructed to renegotiate within six months the salary packages of all insurance agents after the CEO learned to her outrage that they earned more than she did. His success was essential to the company's new strategy, which was based on eliminating discounting from how insurance agents closed contracts and removing all individual bonuses in favor of a collective bonus based on combined results.

Routine

Marek relied heavily on routine, tradition, and stability. He believed that the best way to avoid conflict and reach agreement was to ensure that people knew their roles, the rules, and what was expected of them. He prepared a script well in advance of every meeting and followed it to the letter. He would be methodical and patient. Everything would go fine with the renegotiation so long as everyone conformed to the carefully orchestrated process that shaped the annual review of salaries and conditions.

Usually, Marek appeared unflappable, no matter how much the union representatives gesticulated and banged on the table. While their strong emotions baffled him, he maintained his veneer of composure and professionalism, ensuring that the minutes captured all the details of their concerns and promising to return with a response at the next meeting.

That year was different, though. The unions expected change under the new CEO, and they were busy determining what was non-negotiable, identifying their red lines, and marking out their territory. The head of the main union, who was also new, interrupted Marek's long introductory presentation, questioning when he was going to get to the point. Marek, holding to his established way of doing things, sought to create a constructive atmosphere by focusing initially on process, but the union leader wanted to get to the union's demands as quickly as possible.

Marek's stance infuriated her. Correctly or not, she interpreted his words and actions as those of an arrogant bureaucrat. "He's going to strangle us," she told her colleagues when the meeting adjourned exactly on time. Marek shook her hand sincerely, explaining that lunch had been arranged in the executive dining room and telling her how much he looked forward to getting to know her over the coming months.

Collapse

Marek was quite astute at reading others. He could sense the union leader's need to prove herself, her impatience, and her apparent toughness. But Marek expected her, like so many before her, to come to see things differently once she'd grown tired of her own belligerence and got to know everyone better over many lunches and coffee breaks. He intended to overwhelm her with cordiality and kindness until she was ready to hear what he had in mind.

During the early phase of the negotiations, Marek didn't mention his CEO's most important demands. He worked around the edges, focusing on the fine detail of the existing agreements. Progress was painfully slow and unproductive.

Then, one month into the process, some insurance agents discovered what the CEO was planning and immediately notified the union. Later that day, Marek received a call from the union head. He was informed that the negotiations were being terminated because of bad faith and was accused of playing politics and being manipulative.

While Marek regretted his inability to bring the key issues to the fore earlier in the negotiations, the attack on his integrity hit hard. His stomach burned, and he swallowed another heartburn tablet, dreading the urgent meeting he would have to have with his CEO. How would he explain that he hadn't yet told the unions about the contractual changes? He felt helpless, weak, and desperately angry with himself for disappointing his boss.

Coffee was served. The CEO and CFO sat in silence. The next thing Marek heard was the sound of his heart monitor beeping and the rattle and buzz of the emergency ward.

Compliance

In contrast to a growth-minded leader like Jacinda Ardern, a Snail rarely combines their compassion with courage. In such situations, a Snail like Marek would respond emotionally but also would either find themselves overwhelmed by events or retreat into the shell-like familiarity of the known and routine, avoiding the discomfort of confrontation and censure.

It's this propensity to revert to bureaucracy and doing things by the book that renders Snails' behavior weak. The servility, spinelessness, and self-protection of MP Jim Hacker (played by Paul Eddington) in the BBC show *Yes Minister* captures this well, particularly in Hacker's dealings with the civil service, as embodied by the condescending and manipulative permanent secretary Sir Humphrey Appleby (played by Nigel Hawthorne), and the prime minister. Snails leave a trail of slime behind them.

To thrive, an employee needs to know that their boss has their back, that they expect them to take risks, learn new skills, and influence others. They need someone to root for their success, providing advice and guidance, competing for resources to support their work, and helping resolve conflicts when they arise. They don't want someone who retreats when the going gets tough or meekly complies when confronted by the self-interested guardians of the status quo. That just looks like politics.

The Snail's excessive worrying about what others think means that in times of crisis they stop sharing information, insights, and ideas. And if they find themselves enmeshed in a conspiracy of silence between Hippos and Snails, as the inquiry into the King's Cross fire revealed was the case at the London Underground, Snails become convinced that remaining quiet is preferable to accepting the risks associated with speaking up to a Hippo.

Inevitably, the Snail's conformity and acquiescence are exploited by the loud and the powerful. Peers and direct reports may put up with their meekness and affability, but they won't respect them and will find ways to exploit their weakness, indecision, and inability to enforce clear boundaries and expectations. This situation increases exponentially when Snails find themselves in submissive relationships with Hippos, who have no time for or interest in rules, principles, or values if they don't serve their own needs. Hippos will take advantage of the Snail's service-oriented willingness to follow, listen, and forgive, as well as their inability to negotiate or confront effectively.

Lacking the capacity to protect their teams and compete for the resources they require, Snails inhibit their potential to transform into growth leaders. Over time, regardless of their job titles and positions on the corporate ladder, they lose both influence and responsibility. This outcome throws into question the current trend in leadership literature, which advocates humility, empathy, vulnerability, and selfless service. The relatively new emphasis on so-called soft skills appears to be an understandable reaction to the ego-driven coercion and bossiness of the Hippo that dominated for so long. Snails don't need soft skills or harder shells. They need an independent and confident voice. They need to show integrity and grit, holding others accountable. They need to add candor to their skill set to counter their excessive kindness, authenticity to counter their conviviality, and presence to counter their invisibility. They need proper teeth, a powerful tail, and less slime.

Most modern organizations don't yet subscribe to the growth mindset principles. They remain domains where only the narcissists and self-confident get ahead, trampling on the Snails in the process. But pushed to an extreme, Snails can become resistant and cynical, regressing into Clams.

12

The Clam

What happens when criticism and skepticism are the dominant leadership characteristics that shape organizational culture?

Overview

Clams build much of their personal authority on stern objectivity, expert status, and independence. They're very hard to impress, arrogant even. They go out of their way to undermine alternatives, playing devil's advocate, and thus eroding people's ability to make change happen. They don't perceive what they do as sabotage. Instead, they see themselves as misunderstood protectors of the truth, even though that positions them as outsiders.

Clams are people whose MO is to freeze, block, and blame others. They find safety by sticking to their own beliefs and being skeptical of other people and their beliefs. Their shell is stronger than the Snail's, reflecting their resistance, withdrawal, and avoidance.

The INSEAD professor and psychoanalyst Manfred F.R. Kets de Vries identifies these tendencies in *The Leadership Mystique*, with editions published in 2001 and 2006. His preferred metaphor is the mussel:

> The lowly mussel has a lot to teach us about change and stasis. This mollusk has to make only one major existential decision in life, and that's where it's going to settle down. After making that decision, the mussel cements its head against a rock and stays put for the rest of its life. I've discovered that many people are like that: they're so resistant to change that they might as well be cemented in place. If leaders share that trait—if they suffer from what we might call the "mussel syndrome"—the results can be devastating for their organizations.

Clams, like Kets de Vries's mussels, are individuals who bemoan not being listened to while actively undermining other people's ideas and initiatives. If they haven't been the instigators of change or innovation, they'll direct their energy toward blocking it and thus maintaining the status quo—even if they dislike the status quo. Clams have excess and self-righteous confidence in their own knowledge, ability, and perspective, and will willfully ignore or diminish what their colleagues have to offer. Many Clams pride themselves on being frank, objective, and emotionally detached.

The Clam's cynicism and skepticism are at their most forceful when the Clam feels overwhelmed or threatened. Isolation, distrust, and suspicion feed their sense of self-reliance and need for self-protection. While Clams can harbor strong opinions and ideas about what must change and how, their preference for negativity and criticism freezes or undermines collective action. They fail to grasp that effective change requires allies, confidence, and hope.

Unsurprisingly, Safe2Great research shows that Clams are the least effective leaders and create the lowest level of psychological safety in the workplace. They're also one of the hardest types of leader to coach. Their inability to accept critical feedback and a stubborn belief in their own rightness can make development toward a growth mindset difficult.

Clam traits

- Don't engage with or show interest in other people.
- Claim that trust should be earned and not freely given.
- Assume others are incompetent.
- Consider themselves misunderstood, underappreciated, and disliked.
- Complain that what they do is neither exciting nor challenging.
- Avoid taking risks and stick to the basics.
- Keep their heads down and do not speak up—until threatened.
- Reject responsibility for mistakes.

Unwelcome

Tene peered over the top of her thick-rimmed glasses. "Next time we meet, make sure you bring someone who knows what they're doing," she growled. The members of the project team scurried from the meeting room. Tene was Chief Compliance Enforcer, and her brutality and Medusa-like gaze tended to unnerve her colleagues.

People would prepare for weeks before attending one of her infamous project reviews. She could excoriate the best-prepared plans, subjecting them to her x-ray vision, assessing and picking fault in the most minute details. Although the CEO placed absolute trust in her, even he avoided meeting her on a one-to-one basis whenever possible.

At our first coaching session, Tene informed me, "I don't suffer fools gladly. I've worked very hard to get where I am today, and I'm not going to put up with ignorance. This company is full of happy talk and bad ideas. My job is to make sure not a single dumb idea gets near our production organization. People who speak nonsense or propose stupid ideas deserve to know it." She spoke calmly but with a blistering intensity.

Neither angry nor happy, Tene was consistently pessimistic and suspicious, always alert to the slightest indication of a performance target being missed or an improvement project overrunning. It was all business all the time. She made no time for small talk or the niceties usually associated with human interaction.

"I've never been to the Christmas party in the twenty years I have been here and never will. And don't try to talk to me about soft skills. If I wanted affection, I'd buy a dog, because dogs don't talk. I can't stand it when people talk too much. Why are you here, by the way?"

"Coaching," I said humorlessly.

"Huh, that must be a joke," she mocked.

"No, it's quite serious, actually," I replied as emotionlessly as possible, mirroring her tone as closely as I could.

"I assume you're here to convert me to your growth mindset religion."

"No. I'm here to help."

"Help . . . Hmm. Don't remember asking for that."

"As you know, it was either talk to me or talk to the out-placement company. Apparently, you chose me."

"I chose a coach, not you."

"I know, but nobody else wanted the job."

"That bad, eh?"

"Yep," I replied.

Torture

Tene was difficult to coach. She was clever, deceptive, self-obsessed, and socially deluded. She may have been a member of Mensa, but she couldn't manage to get through a five-year-old's birthday party without offending someone in the family. She was high in intelligence but wholly lacking in empathy and common sense. Her role in the company was protected by her knowledge about, well, everything. She knew she was both untouchable and irreplaceable, and she repaid her tenure by spending an inhuman amount of time and energy sticking her critical nose into anything new. Spelling mistakes were like a speck of mold on her hard cheddar. Numbers never added up.

Now, though, the production head and the rest of the leadership team had had enough. When a second member of Tene's team went on stress leave in less than three months, the senior executives recognized that they had to act, or everyone would suffer. The fact that one of the team members on stress leave was planning legal action with support from their union only brought matters into sharper relief.

According to her direct reports, working for Tene was torture. Nothing was good enough, everything was wrong, and everyone—except Tene, of course—was incompetent. When the head of HR discussed the situation with her, Tene claimed that the employee who had gone on sick leave was weak and unintelligent. Meanwhile, she argued that her team was under-resourced and unappreciated. She even had the gall to complain about being continuously overlooked for the role of senior vice president of Quality.

When the head of HR left the meeting, he was both angry and confused. "That was an insane meeting," he told me when discussing the coaching project. "She's so caught up in her own world, it's impossible to challenge her or get her to see things from another perspective. She wants to be promoted, but when we insist that she needs to broaden her experience before she would be considered a candidate, she refuses and claims that she's too qualified for the role we suggest."

Insecurity

Despite her thick veneer of invulnerability, Tene was deeply insecure about relationships. But you couldn't tell her that. Her default behaviors were suspicion, blame, and disconnection in all interactions save those with a few like-minded friends and colleagues. Her sense of superiority allowed her to deal with some of the narcissists she met in her role. She would criticize, dismiss, and object. If that didn't work, she would attack—directly or indirectly—the other person's competence. Being the smartest person in the room mattered enormously to her. She was obsessed with "idiots," which revealed an inner struggle with her own self-worth and being taken seriously.

Her unwillingness to broaden her skills and experience hampered her chances of promotion. She hid her anxiety about stepping out of her narrow area of expertise by adopting a condescending tone. She'd read all the books on emotional intelligence and leadership, but she dismissed them as pseudo-science and humanistic hogwash. None of them applied to her.

When I was coaching Tene I always felt like I was on the brink of lifting the lid on Pandora's box. I half expected the entire contents of a miserable life to jump out at any moment and engulf me. I could feel the tension while working with her and could understand how futile people found trying to talk to her about her challenges or offering help. But nothing ever popped out. Tene refused sympathy, advice, and recognition. She met my feedback on her strengths with awkward politeness. She was invincible, impenetrable, and yet still strangely vulnerable. It was difficult for me to imagine a professional life that was so cut off from both colleagues and reality.

The coaching process lasted for three months. Tene approached each session with increasingly intricate forms of defense. She wanted desperately to outsmart and outmaneuver me. I ended up finding it rather depressing. Beneath the bravado was self-loathing. Here was a soul crying out for help but imprisoned by her increasingly calcified shell.

Despite what you might think having read Tene's story, breakthroughs with Clams are possible. I have opened their shells on occasions but not without the use of raw negative feedback. I've sometimes winced hearing my own words, but I know that because Clams receive so little feedback, I have a duty to say what I really think and see in the data. They despise softness as a sign of naïvety and see care as a sign of a lack of independence. Tough love is the only way forward.

Resistance

In *The War of Art*, the novelist Steven Pressfield states that "any act that rejects immediate gratification in favor of long-term growth, health, or integrity" will elicit resistance. The same applies to change, innovation, or any ideas that disrupt the Clam's order and cherished best practices—in other words, anything that challenges the Clam's knowledge and organizational familiarity.

Resistance, Pressfield suggests, shouldn't be taken lightly. It's devious, arising from within, fueled by self-righteousness. Those who resist become increasingly detached and more entrenched in the face of opposition. They protect themselves by being abrasive in their interactions with others. When I first met Tene, I could feel this viscerally. Her words were cutting, her manner always tending toward rudeness, sarcasm, and antipathy.

Psychologically, people who are critical and skeptical by default experience disconnection from others. They can be callous and hurtful, even if this isn't always their intention. They lack empathy, often looking on dispassionately while others suffer, without any sign of remorse or intention to intervene. There's a coolness and distance to them that can be just as harmful as the Hippo's volatility, damaging relationships and impairing organizational operation.

By cauterizing their feelings in the short term, the Clam creates a sense of safety for themselves. But persistent emotional inhibition has a long-term numbing effect. The Clam becomes anesthetized, incapable of expressing happiness or sadness, finding no joy or inspiration in what they do or in their occasional interactions with colleagues and clients, unless it involves some intellectual sparring, disagreement, or debate. They're perceived as cold, bored, and uninterested. But when their attention is caught, Clams are disparaging of other people's displays of emotion, which they see as highlighting the weakness of the other's character, their work, or their ideas.

Because Clams are uncooperative, believing in the superiority of their own knowledge and methods over those of their colleagues, they're seen as unconventional and rebellious. They rarely show respect or a sense of common purpose, and therefore find it difficult to mobilize others. While the Clam's independence can serve as a catalyst to innovation, it's more often an expression of their suspicion, distrust, and, in the worst cases, paranoia. Certain of their own genius, Clams believe that others are jealous of them and want to humiliate the Clam with their false kindness and camaraderie. They fear looking stupid or naïve.

In many organizations, despite the relational harm caused by their distance, sarcasm, and cynicism, the toughness of the Clam is considered a useful attribute, particularly during times of uncertainty and transformation. Their skepticism and unflinching ability to scrutinize and question can unearth issues and expose flaws. But the Clam's risk aversion and innate pessimism can quickly kill grand visions and aspirations for positive change. Don't get me wrong. Clams are very committed, determined, and hardworking. The problem is that they have the inverse impact on others, either by making people hate working with them, or sending them on endless goose-chasing tasks to fulfill their need to prove someone wrong.

In *Immunity to Change*, developmental psychologist Robert Kegan and change leadership specialist Lisa Laskow Lahey identify the intertwined and multidimensional aspects of change resistance. These aspects include thwarting challenging aspirations, managing anxiety, and organizing reality. Clams are know-it-alls. It's not unusual for them to spend time criticizing and proving everyone else wrong before revealing their own, long-withheld solution. Meetings are an intellectual game for them, and they have no qualms about using their power and influence to block other proposals and ideas. They impose their knowledge and perspective, managing their own fears, and only allowing change that they find acceptable.

As with the Hippo and the Snail, how the Clam interacts with other people affects an organization culturally, operationally, and, ultimately, financially. I explore this in the next chapter.

13

The Cost of Darkness

What is the impact of protective mindsets?

Control creates coverups

In the most dysfunctional organizations, where leadership demands are unrealistic and the pressure to perform is overwhelming, the need for self-protection among both individuals and teams encourages a lack of cooperation. Consequently, employees withhold information and cover up project failures and malpractice. The reputational damage that ensues when such transgressions are exposed can be fatal for some businesses. And for the companies that do survive, recovery and the rebuilding of trust—not only between colleagues, but between a business and its customers—can take years.

Let's explore some of the most significant costs of the dark side of leadership.

Silence

When I coached Sylvester, the long-suffering project manager who reported to Rashid, he explained how difficult it had been to deal with Rashid's behavior and demands and their effect on his fellow executives.

> Two years of unreasonable criticisms, ridiculous requests, pushback, and overreach. Of course, we knew that there were problems with the product and the new production process. I tried as well as I could to explain it, but the reality was that the steering group was caught in the past. They may have understood the product and manufacturing processes ten years ago, but things had moved on. Early on, I presented the data candidly and honestly, but soon realized that I could not continue.

After the meeting at which Rashid had humiliated Sylvester and his team, Sylvester decided to double-report. One report would be submitted to the steering group, and a more transparent report would be given verbally to the project team. This was a well-intentioned cover-up in the hope that things would work out for the best while the team tried to protect itself from further humiliation.

Unofficially, Sylvester did his best to flag the risks and prepare people for potential problems with the product rollout. He wasn't proud of his approach, but he felt it was better to persist with the project rather than walk away and thought he could use his network within the company to prevent further damage. Unfortunately, despite the wealth of good people around him, he couldn't turn around a situation created by unrealistic expectations and poor decision-making.

The paranoid leader who fears rebellion and loss of control eventually hears only silence. Nobody wants to tell them what's really going on. But those who are silent, who don't challenge and speak truth to power, also bear a burden of responsibility. Their conspiracy of silence and inaction are as harmful as the Hippo's authoritarian behavior.

When organizations reach these depths of hypocrisy, change agents and potential whistleblowers who could make a difference often hold themselves in check, convinced that whatever they do will be futile. Their misgivings and reservations are understandable. Despite the existence of legislation in several countries to protect whistleblowers who report fraud and malpractice, it often proves to be ineffective. For example, a review of the whistleblower protections created in the USA by the 2002 *Sarbanes-Oxley Act* found that the legislation did little to change cultural pressures to maintain silence irrespective of what might have been witnessed. In many cases, whistleblowers were consistently ignored or even attacked for speaking up.

Mistakes and mishaps

People who feel threatened or humiliated stop thinking straight, miss important cues, and lose their concentration. Christine Porath, in *Mastering Community,* cites research supporting this finding: "In a survey of 4,500 doctors and nurses, 71 percent saw a link between disruptive behavior (defined as 'abusive personal conduct,' including condescending, insulting, or rude behavior) and medical errors they knew of, and 27 percent connected such behavior to actual deaths among their patients." She also cites research that shows that doctors stop thinking and get stuck on initial incorrect diagnoses when exposed to rudeness.

My research shows that protective mindsets correlate negatively with psychological safety. Clams are especially guilty of making people feel unsafe—and people experiencing low psychological safety in a team are much more likely to rate the quality of their own work lower.

In *Good Boss, Bad Boss*, Robert Sutton cites research that supports the connection between controlling leadership and poor quality. Perhaps the most important source he cites is W. Edwards Deming, who found that micromanagement, arbitrary performance targets, and a focus on cost-cutting can lead to reduced quality and productivity in manufacturing settings.

Conflict

As I wrote in the analysis of the King's Cross Underground fire, organizations aren't smooth-running machines. They're often full of conflicts, siloed, and rigid. Peace and harmony might be achieved for a while, often with major compromises, but they never last long. Conflicts can be started and exacerbated by many things—change, poor communication, unfair treatment, personality differences, disagreements about goals, confusion about areas of responsibility, and/or competition for resources like time, money, and attention.

Protective mindsets, particularly the Hippo and the Clam, contribute to conflict because of their lack of empathy and care for others. Their conflict styles are either combative or competitive, seeking to win arguments no matter what. Various studies have revealed that employees in the USA each spend around 2.5 hours per week dealing with conflict. For example, in 2017, the Society for Human Resource Management (SHRM) conducted a study on workplace conflict, which found that 95% of US employees have experienced conflict at work, and that managers spend an average of 13% of their time dealing with conflicts. The study estimated that this adds up to an average of 2.8 hours per week per employee, or approximately $359 billion in lost time and productivity annually.

Illegality

Business, politics, and sport are littered with examples of silence, inaction, a distorted sense of loyalty, or simple greed leading to illegality: the world of professional cycling during the height of the EPO era, the Nixon administration's attempts to cover up the Watergate break-in, the emissions scandal involving VW and other car manufacturers, and Danske Bank's involvement in money-laundering, to name only four.

In each case, people did exactly—and sometimes more than—what was asked of them. They cut corners, obfuscated, and lied—either through blind obedience to their leaders or through loyalty to the organization and their colleagues. Frequently, though, they sought to protect themselves and their jobs.

The latter appears to have been the case at Boeing during the buildup to the 737 Max scandal.

Earlier I mentioned David Gelles's book about Jack Welch and how Welch seemed to have contributed to Hippos' ability to stay in power regardless of their sins. Gelles also traces the careers of some of Welch's acolytes from GE as they left their mark on US businesses. For example, he follows Harry Stonecipher to McDonnell Douglas and then to the CEO role at Boeing after the two companies merged in 1997. In the following years, Boeing rapidly became the hero of Wall Street like GE before it, but soon talk of scandals and unethical behaviors emerged. Gelles quotes a former Boeing engineer and union leader who describes the culture change at Boeing after the McDonnell Douglas (ex-GE) leaders arrived: "The company's safety culture was replaced with a culture of financial bullshit, a culture of groupthink." Gelles traces the influence of ex-GE leaders on Boeing's culture, operations, and decisions, explaining in detail how GE's cost-cutting and market-bending practices ultimately led to the two 737 Max crashes in Ethiopia and Indonesia which killed over three hundred people.

Before the merger with McDonnell Douglas, Boeing had a culture that valued engineering excellence, quality, innovation, and open communication between executives and staff. Following the merger, the organizational focus shifted to share value, profit generation, speed to market, cost efficiencies, and competition with aerospace rivals. Shortcuts were taken, knowledge was lost because of departures and layoffs, and employee loyalty was destroyed. Executives didn't want their decisions challenged. People no longer felt able to "stop the line" and raise quality issues. Whistleblowers lost their jobs and safety standards consequently dropped.

Against this toxic background, executives pushed for the rapid rollout of an aircraft that could challenge Airbus's A320neo market dominance. They wanted something that would require minimal scrutiny from the Federal Aviation Administration (FAA) and no additional training for pilots. The decision was taken to introduce a new version of the Boeing 737 model, and to do everything possible to minimize attention on new design features, including the existence of a maneuvering characteristics augmentation system (MCAS).

A Congress inquiry later revealed that Boeing put the planes in the air fully aware of design flaws and of the need to train pilots on the new MCAS. Corporate greed took precedence over product quality and safety. Yet it carried a substantial cost. In September 2022, Boeing was fined $200 million and former CEO Dennis Muilenburg fined $1 million for their deception.

Poor mental health

The organizations we belong to and the cultures we find our-selves a part of have an enormous impact on our mindset and our mental health. We're already cognitively and collabora-tively stretched, so any additional exposure to incivility and abusive practices can lead to burnout or depression. In my research, Hippos and Clams are poor at meeting employees' emotional needs. They lack the ability to show care because of their narcissism, detachment, or arrogance. Snails can appear so lacking in self-respect that their caring behaviors can seem disingenuous, or they fail to protect or defend employees from unreasonable bosses, peers, and customers. When Hip-pos lead organizations, their disregard for civility and respect usually becomes codified in the organizations' structures and operational processes, perpetuating old practices that deny autonomy and exploration, relying instead on control, exces-sive supervision, and bureaucratic rigidity.

Employees who are bullied, abused, and treated with a lack of respect tend to enter a self-perpetuating negative spi-ral. They are subjected to aggressive behaviors and then mir-ror those behaviors when they interact with workmates and customers, transforming their experience of powerlessness into momentary exercises of power. They pass their stress on, becoming toxic themselves because of how their boss treats them. Toxic behavior spreads quickly because of physical proximity, according to Sutton.

At a personal level, internal corporate pressures and acts of incivility have an impact on health. In a 2015 *HBR* article titled "Proof That Positive Work Cultures Are More Produc-tive," Emma Seppälä and Kim Cameron note the American Psychological Association (APA) has found that health-care costs in the United States are nearly 50% higher in high-pressure organizations.

The American Psychological Association estimates that more than $500 billion is siphoned off from the U.S. economy because of workplace stress, and 550 million workdays are lost each year due to stress on the job. Sixty percent to 80% of workplace accidents are attributed to stress, and it's estimated that more than 80% of doctor visits are due to stress. Workplace stress has been linked to health problems ranging from metabolic syndrome to cardiovascular disease and mortality.

Luckily, in every culture assessment I've conducted since 2005, I've found that Dolphins and dolphin pods always seem to find ways to work effectively, even in dysfunctional, toxic organizations. Inevitably, they have a resourceful, growth-minded leader who creates an umbrella for them, keeping out toxic behavior while still being able to deliver on key responsibilities. This has proved to me that growth leadership can come from anywhere and need not be top-down. It also shows that the immediate manager is the most important factor in shaping a team's mental health. Perhaps this finding is linked to Porath's study of over twenty thousand people around the world. She found that being treated with respect is considered more important than anything else in the workplace. It's valued above recognition, appreciation, feedback, and learning opportunities: "Civility lifts people. We'll get people to give more and function at their best if we're civil. Incivility chips away at people and their performance. It robs people of their potential."

Quiet quitting

The COVID-19 pandemic accelerated one of the most significant mega-trends in the workplace over the last thirty years: the hyper-individualistic approach to the relationship between an organization and its employees. However, this approach has developed in parallel with an unprecedented hyper-connectivity of work itself. We have more matrices, more cross-functionality, and more joint ventures and partnerships than ever. The paradox is that while we need more collaboration and community, most leaders seem to lead and manage on a one-to-one basis.

In 2020, we went home to work and most of us soon realized that we wanted to stay there. In 2022, Microsoft and Gallup discovered that employees like hybrid work and feel it makes them more productive, but bosses aren't convinced: 87% of employees report being productive working remotely, and 88% of leaders are dubious about the accuracy of this claim. Satya Nadella refers to this difference as "productivity paranoia" among bosses.

My interpretation of this data is slightly different to Nadella's. I think he and others are either unaware of or underestimating how antisocial, demoralizing, and Hippo-dominated workplaces are. There are far too many discouraging and negative face-to-face interactions at the office. When we're online, we can turn off the camera or just work on something else. We can rebel or resist in our pajamas.

It's much easier to be a Hippo at the office. When everyone is in the mud pool with you, it's much easier to control them without resorting to overt displays of power—and as we know, most Hippos like to keep their dirty, controlling ways hidden. Deniability is an important tool in the Hippo toolbox. Domination is most often manifested physically by speaking loudly, displaying anger, interrupting others, mocking, glaring, and invading personal space. These behaviors are only effective when people are in the same room. Watching a Hippo go about their usual aggressive behaviors online with too much back light, a poor microphone, and everyone else on mute is almost comical. Perhaps it's a form of poetic justice?

Passive aggression

When people experience injustice, they find ways to fight back or get even. The correlation between abusive leadership and theft, vandalism, and absenteeism has been demonstrated in research published in the *Journal of Applied Psychology*. Poor leadership over time creates high levels of disconnection, passive-aggressiveness, and apathy. At least, that's what I've found in organizational units with high scores on the Clam operating modes. Rumor-mongering, backstabbing, and disparaging remarks at the water cooler are all behavioral characteristics of people who have shifted into resistance. These behaviors are also particularly present in organizations going through changes, mergers, and other disruptions.

Resistance is the focus of most change leadership training. However, controlling leaders, who are the main drivers of resistance, are rarely one of the topics discussed. Leaders are obsessed with people who are "change resistant," despite the evidence that people resist poor change management, not change itself. Identifying and labeling people as resistant justifies more control and coercion. So the merry-go-round of control and complacency continues to turn.

When I'm a co-navigator on the change journey, I am committed. When I'm a comfy passenger, I comply. When I'm a hostage, I resist.

The No Hippo Zone

I've had the opportunity to observe lots of businesses as an outsider on the inside. I continue to be surprised by how often individuals, teams, and organizations fail to see how dysfunctional they are. These organizations cling to their established ways of working even when they are confronted with and accept the need to change. I attribute this blindness to five common characteristics of "hippo-critical" organizations.

- Leaders can't see or don't care about the impact of their own behavior.
- Employees don't share what they're experiencing.
- There's a big gap between what leaders say and what they actually do.
- Leaders ignore or reject feedback about their impact or behavior.
- Employees don't believe in what they're doing.

When I introduce the concept of growth mindset to an organization, it's often dismissed as a soft option when compared with the Hippo's tough and demanding approach, the Snail's rigid compliance, or the Clam's skepticism. A growth-oriented leadership style is misunderstood as friendly and playful, when it's really about being constructively challenging and candid, stretching people and what they're capable of.

There's nothing easy about growth mindset. Protective mindsets offer far simpler approaches to leadership. For Hippos, it's easier to control others than to show trust in them. For Snails, it's easier to be nice than to hold people accountable. For Clams, it's easier to criticize and challenge than to contribute to a common solution. All three might even get a big thrill from their behaviors.

As I mentioned, the Hippo was inspired by Sutton's *The No Asshole Rule*. Over the years since the book was first published, many companies have adopted Sutton's ideas as a code of conduct for their organizational culture. While some choose to use the milder expression "the No Jerk Rule," the point is the same. Toxic people need to tame their inner hippo or go, and it looks like the corporate world is slowly catching on. HubSpot, Netflix, Zappos (now a part of Amazon), and IDEO, for example, explicitly reject the idea that you have to be a jerk to be successful.

These companies are still in the minority, though. In an MIT *Sloan Management Review* article titled "How to Fix a Toxic Culture," Donald Sull and Charles Sull, co-founders of CultureX, report that over 90% of North American CEOs and CFOs recognize that improving their organizations' corporate culture would have a positive impact on performance and financial return. Most acknowledge that their cultures are unhealthy, yet they've done little to remedy the situation. This lack of action is partly down to a general lack of effective methods to tackle toxicity, harassment, and exclusion in the workplace. The Safe2Great method is designed to fill this gap.

In the companies where I've consulted, we've run campaigns based on the No Hippo Zone, and it's arguably the most memorable thing I've created. What started as a joke became a phenomenon—in at least one company where the concept was rolled out effortlessly and surprisingly quickly, it continues to shape how teams set expectations and give feedback on behaviors. We sell a lot of Dolphin badges ("Catch people at their best"), but they aren't as popular as the No Hippo Zone badges and stickers.

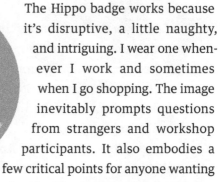

The Hippo badge works because it's disruptive, a little naughty, and intriguing. I wear one whenever I work and sometimes when I go shopping. The image inevitably prompts questions from strangers and workshop participants. It also embodies a few critical points for anyone wanting to implement a no asshole rule. First, you can't use rude language to create a more civil culture. It's disingenuous to say "jerk" or "asshole" and in the same breath promote respect for others. Second, humor reduces defense mechanisms. The metaphor makes it easier to talk about very difficult subjects like toxicity, exclusion, or harassment. Third, people hate to be lectured to about their behaviors. It's patronizing and often monstrously hippo-critical.

But the need to change culture in a team and organization cannot be overstated. Identifying and replacing unhealthy Hippo, Clam, and Snail behaviors with healthy Dolphin habits is integral to the Safe2Great change process. Workplace stress, a product of low psychological safety and high pressure, is also a key contributor to voluntary turnover. In a March 2022 *MIT Sloan Management Review* article, "Why Every Leader Needs to Worry About Toxic Culture," Donald Sull, Charles Sull, William Cipolli, and Caio Brighenti draw on Glassdoor data taken from 1.3 million reviews to highlight the attritional consequences when leaders are disrespectful, noninclusive, unethical, cutthroat, and abusive: people leave their tyrannical bosses, toxic colleagues, and panopticon-like work environment as soon as they find alternative employment.

14

Summary

Why do we all need to change to create a growth-minded culture?

Before moving on to the next section of the book, I want to highlight two key points.

Each protective mindset requires a unique journey toward a growth mindset. Hippos will need to care as fiercely about people as they do about getting things done. Snails will need to care as strongly about getting things done as they do about helping others. Clams will need to become as strongly attached to the team and common purpose as they are to their individuality and uniqueness of thought. When they achieve these things, they can transform into Dolphins.

If we notice someone acting like a Snail, we need to consider for a moment whether they're being themselves or finding a way to deal with a Hippo. When people are subjected to continuous control and criticism by their leader, they may fight back or they may cope by seeking to please the leader and conform to their demands. A second coping strategy is to become a Clam by seeking to undermine and resist, demonstrating passive-aggressive behavior, and blaming others for errors and failures. The lesson here is that behind some Snails and Clams, there's a Hippo lurking, eyes and snout just visible above the mud.

So, how do we change the direction chosen by the Hippos, Snails, and Clams? Is it possible to help them metamorphose into Dolphins, or at least start moving along the protective-growth continuum?

In a tweet posted on September 2, 2022, the organizational psychologist Adam Grant observed, "People who never let go of their views never evolve. Growth is not just about embracing new ideas. It's also about rethinking old ones. Refusing to change your mind is a decision to stop learning."

Becoming a Dolphin means letting go of what makes you feel powerful, safe, or unique right now. It means moving out of your comfort zone and into the discomfort zone. It means finding new strengths in the six growth principles. In Part III, I describe how to do this.

Transformation

What is the new psychology of leadership?

How do we learn to see the world
and our place in it more accurately?

What do we need to accept about ourselves
and the world to grow our mindset?

What do we need to do to let go of protective
mindsets and develop a growth mindset?

How do we catalyze team and organizational
change to support personal development?

How do we balance the bright and dark side
into a pathway for HR and senior leaders
to follow in developing great organizations?

15

Safe to Great

Every person, organization, and even society reaches a point at which they owe it to themselves to hit refresh–to reenergize, renew, reframe, and rethink their purpose.
SATYA NADELLA, *Hit Refresh*

Safety first

I started this book with a story about diving that highlights how creating psychological safety is essential to achieving something great. I then outlined the four ages of our time– Green, Globotic, Caring, and Digital Enlightenment–showing how they bring with them seriously negative consequences, but also the opportunity for something great to arise (e.g., the "wonderful recovery" envisaged by David Attenborough). To realize great outcomes in the four ages, we need leaders, companies, unions, and governments to create safety at work and at home. As safety becomes more entrenched, it's possible to imagine growing mindsets, as well as implementing many other activities, to embrace the threats, mitigate the hardships, and then realize a recovery through thriving new ecosystems.

I haven't hidden my social and moral agenda. I want a fairer and more equal world. I want to reduce the amount of stress, burnout, and mental illness caused by poor workplaces and toxic bosses. I'm not alone in thinking that real human progress, rather than pure economic growth, requires a shift in economic paradigm from mining to farming. Without good growth—that is, a just transition into the Green and Globotic Ages—we won't be able to change quickly enough, if at all. Without good growth, the darker sides of the four ages will reduce psychological safety so much that there's a real chance of our organizations and societies unraveling.

In this sense, Safe2Great implies psychological safety not only at work but also across our communities and our planet. 🖐

We also need to become newsmart. We can achieve this through better and more inclusive human-human collaboration, but we also need to become corobotic and enhance our intelligence and productivity via smart machines. These are promising pathways to address workplace burnout primarily driven by cognitive and collaborative overload, as long as the productivity gains made by smarter thinking and working aren't absorbed by even great demands on workers.

Mindset is central to how we weave strands of thinking, feeling, acting, and being into a coherent self. For me, a growth mindset provides a more adaptive and prosocial way of organizing your mind. It can help you grow with the challenges, to do more and be more, and prevent you getting stuck and un-growing. It also enables you to bring out the best in others via relational potential. My growth mindset is about harnessing and contributing to collective intelligence, collaborative effort, and common purpose.

In Part I, The Bright Side, I presented commitment as an alternative to controlling leadership. I explored the secrets of success of Satya Nadella and other Dolphins in bringing about growth and change. Commitment really is at the core of outstanding performance. Dolphins can create hot spots that multiply relational potential and team intelligence.

I explored how people in HROs learn and stay safe in high-risk work environments like the flight deck of an aircraft carrier by listening heedfully. I argued that speaking up reduces screwing up and that hierarchical organizations need to pay close attention to how status affects psychological safety. Commitment used to mean the team members' commitment to companies and their customers, but in ecosystems we'll need to build commitment to a common purpose that's bigger than any organization.

My exploration of the future of health care highlighted the extraordinary potential of deep learning to improve outcomes for patients and increase productivity for physicians, who are overwhelmed and burning out. However, we'll need to find a much better balance between how we share these productivity gains so that deep empathy and care can be developed in health care and in many other human-facing occupations. If not, we risk cynicism and increased burnout.

I then presented my six growth leadership principles: Transform, Aim High, Explore, Go High, Lift Others Up, and Team Up. The most common threads in this part of the book were how autonomy benefits innovation, quality, and performance and how psychological safety allows people to become motivated by dreams and aspirations rather than fears. A third thread was the relational nature of a growth mindset and the importance of collaboration in all aspects of work in the future. We really do multiply or diminish the capabilities and intelligence of others depending on our mindset. As implied by the Caring Age, we must demonstrate more care as leaders at all levels of the organization. Bringing people together via a common purpose is the fourth thread. Success in the ecosystems of the future will require companies and their leaders to be activists for causes that improve the environment and human prosperity.

In Part II, The Dark Side, I explored the three protective mindsets (the Hippo, Snail, and Clam) and how one mindset in particular, the Hippo, creates an unsafe and unfair playing field. Essentially, all organizations are struggling to release themselves from various forms of controlling leadership, controlling technologies, or both. Historically, we prefer bossy bosses and people who follow the script. Growing requires us to disrupt bossy bosses and enable people to use their wits.

Through three stories, I illustrated how Hippos, Snails, and Clams think, feel, and act. An important thread in this part of the book was how operating in protective ways makes you feel safe, and can even induce feelings of being thrilled, but makes others insecure, indifferent, or angry. These negative consequences are hidden from our view by confirmation bias but can lead to substantial career derailments or mistakes. Rashid found himself with a major business failure. Marek collapsed at work due to stress and burnout. Tene was facing dismissal for toxic behavior toward direct reports.

Part II concluded with a review of the most significant costs of the dark side of leadership. Hippos and Clams have the most negative consequences for employees, frequently triggering conflicts, silence, mistakes, illegal acts, poor mental health, and resistance. Snails fail to protect their people from these consequences, and this leads to lower psychological safety despite Snails being generous and nice. Finally, I highlighted the need to implement a No Hippo Zone in your teams and organization as a whole. Culture has an important role to play in supporting personal development. If we don't create growth-minded, hippo-free communities, we won't get far developing our leaders or employees.

What then is the new psychology of leadership?

A new psychology of leadership

The four ages present unique and rapidly deepening challenges. And we're up against the clock. We have ten years, maybe less, to make substantial progress on all four fronts simultaneously. To succeed, I believe we need a new psychology of leadership that reflects the now and the future of work. We have new questions to ask, new solutions to forge, and perhaps most importantly, a new growing mindset to develop.

As leaders in the Green Age, we must ask, How can we contribute to saving the planet? How does our current company purpose align with the necessities and opportunities of the Green Age? How do we mobilize resources and inspire changes in consumer behavior, government policy, and business practices fast enough to avoid the extremes of climate change? How do we change fast enough to prevent climate disaster? How do we unite and align people and organizations across ecosystems via a strong purpose and new forms of cross-business collaboration? How do we learn to work with nature?

As leaders in the Globotic Age, we must ask, How do we integrate robots and AI into our business processes in a meaningful way? Must we redesign everything? How do we improve decision-making quality and speed with the help of machine learning? How do we build inclusive teams that can work locally, remotely, and globally in a seamless manner? What processes and services require the human touch? How do we learn new things? Do we need to learn at all? Will AI do the learning for us?

As leaders in the Caring Age, we must ask, How do we develop and retrain people faster than ever? How do we act as good citizens when we have to let people go? What promises can we realistically make to new employees about their careers? How can we reduce the gap in pay between executives and employees, and between men and women? How do we reduce cynicism and disengagement by showing real commitment to employee welfare? How do we create psychological safety and good mental health? How do we create more inclusive leadership and teams?

As leaders in the Digital Enlightenment Age, we must ask, How can we verify that the machines are right? How do we create confidence in communication and news in light of the prevalence of deep fakes? How do we avoid the temptation to use technology to control everything and everyone? How do we make algorithms transparent and accountable to human priorities? How do we give customers and employees more control over their data? How do we use technology to make our workplaces more human, more empathetic, collaborative, and creative?

The search for a quick fix

Growth mindset has become one of those magical expressions in corporate presentations like customer-oriented, Lean, Agile, and change-ready, to name but four. Just saying it can lead to an improvement in the share price. In a recent discussion with a client, I asked why growth mindset was now on the agenda in their company of over forty thousand employees. The answer was both surprising and revealing: "When the Chairman announced we were going to develop a growth mindset, the share price bumped up 10%!" I don't know whether this story is true or urban myth, but the response emphasizes to me that implementing growth mindset requires us to manage cynicism. Conversely, it also suggests that there's an opportunity to use the poster-child success of growth mindset at Microsoft to get important political actors on board. But as with most buzzwords, the attractiveness of the expression belies the challenging and uncomfortable developmental process needed to bring about real change.

When I work with organizations or individuals on transformational projects, many leaders are looking for a quick fix—like dieters looking for instant weight loss while they continue to enjoy their calorie-laden favorite treats. They want the bullet points, the activities, the communication package, all before they've taken real ownership of an issue. But learning to control ourselves and choosing constructive ways to talk and engage respectfully with others takes practice—and months of frustration and backslides—before it becomes automatic and sincere. Words, especially buzzwords, mean almost nothing. When it comes to behavioral or cultural change, seeing is believing. Therefore, the communication package involves the leaders themselves. To paraphrase Mahatma Gandhi, they must become the change they want to bring to the world.

Leaders' low appetite for critical information and challenge is a constant barrier to any change project, and this is especially true when implementing a growth mindset, as leaders are the target of the change. They need to change their behaviors. And they rarely travel along the Safe2Great path without a fight. Added pressure comes in the form of quarterly results, reorganizations, and unexpected events in the business, all of which will distract, disrupt, and derail a growth mindset project quite regularly. Implementing a growth mindset takes years not weeks, and staying committed to the process is one of the biggest challenges leaders will face.

Reinventing culture and the psychology of leadership requires embedding new practices and principles, but also quickly working out a way for the ideas to reproduce and thrive. Evolution is about successful reproduction, not just effectiveness. You need a good idea, but you also need people living and continuously reinforcing your principles. As leaders come and go on their career merry-go-round, we need a solid group of teachers, role models, and ambassadors actively preaching, showing the way, and improving accountability and transparency.

To guide leaders and organizations through this process of discovery, responsibility, renewal, and growth, I devised a four-phase model:

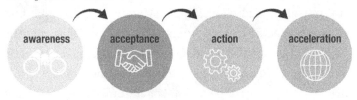

AWARENESS: Seeing things critically and accurately and letting go of false assumptions.

ACCEPTANCE: Taking responsibility for the current state and realizing you can change things.

ACTION: Overcoming the consciously incompetent phase and achieving mastery.

ACCELERATION: Sharing, teaching, and coaching others to develop a growth mindset.

I said in the introduction that this isn't a how-to book or a textbook, but I recognize that you might need some inspiration to get started on the Safe2Great approach and work toward developing a growth mindset. Let me share my four-stage development model and how one Hippo turned into a Dolphin.

Awareness

Seeing clearly comes first.

We won't get far until we throw off the shroud of false positivity that's become so common in leadership, team, and organizational development. Most organizations cling to a veneer of corporate values or employee branding and forget to apply critical thinking to their behaviors and culture. I often ask senior leadership teams, "If everything that's poor, ineffective, and slow in your organization is traceable back to the way the senior leaders behave, what must this team do differently?"

We must see what's really going on and how we're contributing to it before we can transform ourselves, let alone anyone else. We need awareness. We need to discover our blind spots, our unconscious commitments, and our knee-jerk reactions. Otherwise, we'll be operating in a protective rather than growth mode. Growth leaders realize that they're part of the problem. Protective leaders deny their responsibility or blame others and seek to explain things as if they're separate from the problem.

Writing for *McKinsey* about the irrational side of change management, Carolyn Dewar and Scott Keller note that most leaders overestimate how aligned they are with any new strategy they implement. In my work, I've made a similar and important discovery about self-awareness: over 60% of leaders rate themselves completely differently to how others rate them based on our Growth Mindset Leadership 360 assessment. This means that most leaders have no idea how they impact their direct reports, peers, and bosses. My study also revealed that many highly effective woman leaders totally underestimate their positive impact on others, a finding that should trigger alarm bells in recruitment departments everywhere. When women rate themselves so poorly—believing themselves to have a strong protective mindset, when their direct reports and peers rate them as having a growth mindset—it influences their likelihood of being hired or promoted to senior leadership roles.

The dark side of leadership and organizations is an uncomfortable truth. My experience is that people struggle significantly with the critical ideas behind it. However, we must understand that the biggest barriers to growth for any organization are the restricting, inefficient, and demotivating practices so many of us inflict on each other. The ease with which teams and relationships become demoralizing rather than uplifting continues to surprise people. Yet they dismiss the findings or shift blame onto someone else when confronted with survey data that makes these problems both concrete and personal. Never underestimate the power of denial and defensiveness when our self-concepts are challenged. Sadly, some Hippos are delighted to discover that they really are as "badass" as they think they are. It simply confirms their preferred operating model, based loosely on the principles of the survival of the fittest.

Part of the awareness process is surfacing implicit theories about how to create success, and redefining these explicitly in a way that aligns with growth mindset principles. As leaders, we can't make real progress if we don't embrace the growth mindset principles to at least some extent. This might look like reconsidering our own values and principles for success. What kinds of leadership have encouraged us? What kinds of relationships helped us grow or succeed? When we have these models in mind, it's useful to evaluate how much we live up to them on a daily basis and in what way.

One barrier that often arises here is a lack of detailed insight into our own behavior. Leaders can't explain why or how they lead at a behavioral level. They lead habitually, blindly, and unintentionally. Learning to identify healthy and unhealthy habits, see hidden negative impacts on others, and lead intentionally are three growth mindset practices.

Of course, you can't just walk into a room or join a video call and tell someone to instantly change who they are and what they believe. An individual must want to change (they need acceptance too), and anyone assisting them through change must be mindful of the context in which they operate. I've discovered through my coaching and consultancy experiences that it's possible to help people gain greater understanding of their own behavior, of what underlies it, and of how other people perceive and respond to them. Such insights can be the catalyst for change. Transformation even.

John is a tall, strong, talkative Iowan in his mid-forties. When he first heard about the growth mindset concept, he thought that it described him and what he valued in leadership perfectly. John likes to win, challenging himself and others. He was understandably frustrated, therefore, when the results from his Growth Mindset 360 assessment didn't fit with how he scored himself in his Growth Mindset Self Test. He learned that other people found him controlling, overly competitive, and too quick to judge or instruct. Members of his team felt that he didn't enable their own development.

While John did demonstrate some of the growth principles, such as Aim High, Go High, and Lift Others Up, his results were below average compared to leaders in our global benchmark. His scores as a Clam and Snail were average or slightly below average (which is a good thing). When he discovered that he scored well above average as a Hippo, he became defensive, struggling to reconcile how he saw himself as a Dolphin and others saw him as a Hippo. He'd overestimated his positive impact and underestimated how negatively people experienced working with him.

During our first coaching session, John expressed surprise at how poorly his colleagues rated his listening skills. I had to point out to him that he'd spent the first fifteen minutes of our call talking, without allowing me to set the agenda. He paused for the first time during our conversation, taking some time to absorb what I'd said.

John is impatient. He's a go-getter who unthinkingly takes the lead. He interrupts people who are slow to get his point or who offer different perspectives and ideas. John backs himself. He's often right, and he likes to prove people wrong when they don't think he can deliver. He likes to be accountable. John is also a storyteller, and he talks himself and his results up, because winners like him are proud of their achievements.

When I asked John about his strengths, he provided a long list with lots of examples of how he'd utilized them. But when I followed up with an inquiry about his weaknesses, he was silent. It was as if he'd never considered the possibility that he could have any weaknesses. It was clear to me that John had a Hippo mindset, and that he invariably stuck to what he knew, repeating the familiar over and over.

The questions I ask the people I coach about their strengths and weaknesses help me understand how self-aware they are. When they respond, I try not to interrupt, merely encouraging them with brief comments. The longer they talk about their strengths—and the fewer weaknesses they acknowledge—the more likely it is that I'm listening to a Hippo or, possibly, a Clam. Those who claim to have few strengths but numerous weaknesses are usually Snails. Dolphins, by contrast, are thoughtful about both their strengths and weaknesses. They tend to talk about luck rather than design, displaying gratitude and humility. The stories each person recounts and the examples they use tell me much about their mindset. As I wrote earlier, mindset is partly fact but mostly story. While I listen, I'm trying to discover whether people are treating my questions with suspicion or openness, talking themselves up or down, or looking for excuses or someone else to blame.

The less I put into the conversation, the more I discover what people are projecting into the space created by my short questions. John easily filled that space with his words. He told a good story, one that was finely crafted and far too polished.

You cannot complete the Awareness phase until:
· you understand the gap (or not) between your self-image and how others see you,
· you develop a more complex understanding of your own mindset, and
· you begin to see connections between what people do and how others respond.

Acceptance

John thought he knew what his clients needed. Funnily enough, it was exactly what he had to sell, and he was good at closing those deals. But times were changing, and he was being asked to lead the transition to solution selling. John's boss told me that John was now expected to sell to more senior people, discover emergent needs, and find customized solutions that created value. It was now about developing long-term relationships with clients, not making slick sales pitches.

When I suggested to John that he relied too heavily on assumptions instead of taking the time to learn what both his customers and his team wanted, he was offended. I explained that senior clients would expect him to show his confidence and expertise by listening rather than telling. If he did all the talking when meeting smart customers, he'd be seen as incompetent. This small observation was the key to shifting the conversation from a protective operating mode to a growth one.

John became reflective and curious, willing to show vulnerability and take risks. He started asking questions, responding to what he was hearing. He then began sharing experiences that showed him in a less flattering light, highlighting areas where he lacked certainty and confidence. John confessed to being daunted by the prospect of speaking to customers who were clearly better educated than him. He didn't want to be thought unintelligent.

The turning point for John was being open about how and what he wanted to improve. After our first debrief he showed the results to his team and asked for feedback and pointers to other areas of focus that he might not have considered. John also "buddied up" with a trusted peer to observe his team meetings and gather anonymous observations about his working methods.

Buddying up is a great way to explore blind spots, try new things, and find the support to go through a challenging development process. John's success was in part driven by the work he did with his "buddy." They participated together on our Leading Others with Growth Mindset program, where we put everyone into peer-coaching pairs. The work they did over the following year together exemplified how best to transform mindsets.

As part of my coaching process, I invite people to journal regularly. Writing down reflections, questions, thoughts, and observations accelerates mindset growth considerably. This approach is inspired by narrative psychological techniques. When we *think* about ourselves and others, we can have inconsistent or contradictory thoughts without noticing them. When we speak or write about ourselves in coaching, we're forced to put our thoughts into a linear structure that often reveals disconnects between values, beliefs, and actions. I call this process *mindset mapping*. Aligning your values, beliefs, and actions is crucial.

You cannot complete the Acceptance phase until:
· you value and want to take responsibility for weaknesses and blind spots,
· you set development goals and choose situations and relationships where you want to change your behavior, and
· you're willing to ask for help.

Action

In my sessions with John over the following months, he went about developing a growth mindset in a disciplined and determined way. He set goals, practiced hard, and monitored his progress, just as he'd done when playing football or studying at college. That streak of competitiveness was still there, and he still wanted to compare his progress to others'. That was how he'd achieved success in the past, and he found it difficult to let go of what had served him well.

John made a greater effort to listen to his team and his clients. He felt uncomfortable letting others do the talking at team meetings and fielding questions from clients about issues he was unaware of or didn't fully understand. But he found that being honest about not having answers helped build trust, and that he and the clients could learn together. This strengthened their professional relationship in a surprising way for John.

The key challenge during the Action phase is overcoming the experience of being "consciously incompetent." When people make the shift from telling people what to do to asking questions and soliciting input, they may not achieve the results they're aiming for because they aren't accustomed to asking questions and so don't frame their questions in a way that will solicit the answers they need. At first, the questions may not elicit any answers. Our questions may not be powerful enough, and people interpret our questions based on their current expectations about us. They may not think we actually want to hear what they have to say. Growth means doing something different *and* shifting people's perceptions. If people consider us a Clam, for example, they'll respond with caution or disregard us entirely when we first introduce growth-minded questions, which are associated with encouragement rather than suspicion.

Perceptions are harder to shift than behaviors. So, an important technique in the Action phase is sharing our change in mindset like John did. We should acknowledge that we're a Clam, for example, but that we want to change, to develop a growth mindset, ask more open questions, and show more interest in what people think. We can put the Lift Others Up principle into effect, recognizing the issues with our past behavior, apologizing for that behavior, inviting others to contribute their ideas, listening to them, and demonstrating that we care. Becoming more intentional and explicit about our mindset in our communication with others is vital to this process.

Change is a team sport. If we want to change our behaviors and mindset, we need to involve others. We require their candid feedback, their support when we're struggling, and their observations when we try something new. We need to watch and learn from growth-minded people and replicate how they do things, and learn to observe how people with protective approaches fail to build commitment.

When I'm coaching leaders and teams, I'm often told that I'm asking leaders to be politically correct. That isn't accurate. My goal is to align emotion with intention in the way people communicate with each other. If we're going to have respectful *and* powerful communication, we must use words, emotions, and body language far more explicitly. Most leaders are hopeless communicators because they don't master these three things. Instead, they end up forcing people to accept their point of view by being rude and angry.

You cannot complete the Action phase until:

· you've shared your development goals and ambition to grow your mindset,
· you've passed the "consciously incompetent" phase in developing new habits, and
· you can notice protective mindsets in the moment and choose growth.

Acceleration

After ten months, at John's request, we conducted another Growth Mindset Leadership 360 assessment, incorporating feedback from his clients this time. He'd made significant progress, improving his effectiveness as a leader. In his report, team members made qualitative comments about his ability to now involve others in problem-solving, delegate responsibility, and coach others. Customers experienced John as high on integrity and honesty, willing to help, and committed to their business.

A humbler, energized, yet still very determined John attended our debriefing session after the second 360 review. Clearly, he was taming his inner Hippo. He was making good progress, applying what he'd learned not only at work but in his home life too, but recognized that he still had some way to go.

He restructured his meetings with the sales team to make them more about growth than pure information sharing. One-on-one meetings became more about learning and aspirations and less about problems and advice. He'd even discussed with his own boss ways to align compensation better with risk-taking, learning, and growth. He got a "no," but hadn't given up on the idea. His boss did agree to start working on growth mindset in his leadership team, though.

Growth mindset had become part of how John spoke about work. He used the language of the six growth principles to remind people to step out of their comfort zone and grow. He started monthly sessions with his own team to teach and learn more about growth mindset. He became a teacher of growth mindset.

By the end of our second round of coaching, he realized that there's no obvious end point to a growth mindset journey. It's a process of developing and realizing a vision of a different self, a different organization, and a different world. It's about the direction in which we travel rather than any point of arrival.

You cannot complete the Acceleration phase until:

- you change restricting structures, processes, and systems to reinforce growth,
- you begin teaching and coaching others to develop their mindset, and
- you create communities of people who regularly meet to support a culture for growth.

Into the woods

Developing a growth mindset can be born out of adversity and failure, but it also can be a proactive desire to change. To illustrate proactive personal growth, INSEAD professors Stewart Black and Hal Gregersen use the example of professional golfer Tiger Woods in their book *It Starts with One*. Woods had already enjoyed a stellar amateur career when he turned professional in 1996. The following year he won his first Major title at the Masters in a record-breaking performance that saw him leading the field by twelve shots. To date, he's won fifteen Majors, over 120 tournaments on the US and European Tours combined, and numerous other titles around the world. He is acknowledged as one of the greatest golfers in history. But these statistics tell only part of the story of his success.

Not long after the first of his five victories at the Masters, Woods and his coach began to work on changing his golf swing in a bid to improve his game. This decision, which surprised rivals and commentators alike, involved a drawn-out process that initially had a detrimental impact on his performance and, by extension, his income from the sport. He experienced the phase of being consciously incompetent. Soon, however, his willingness to learn and explore rather than to rely solely on what had worked in the past began to bear fruit, with Woods again dominating the sport, winning numerous titles and awards.

However, with growing self-knowledge of his body's mechanics and the requirements for longevity in his sport, Woods embarked on another reinvention process in the early 2000s. He wanted to grow rather than simply fade away as a new generation of golfers joined the Tour. Again, there was a drop-off in success and earnings before another bounce back.

As he's aged, navigating the effects of off-course personal dramas, on-course injuries, and the aftermath of a devastating car crash, Woods has continued to grow, admittedly with some major moments of un-growth, remaining competitive in the sport well into his mid-forties.

The third path

This book contains big hopes, uncomfortable truths, and a joke or two. That's the growth mindset way. That's my way. I wanted to show you both what great looks like and how we can only escape ordinariness by learning to identify the protective mindsets that keep us safe, thrill us, and hold us back.

I believe leaders, HR practitioners, consultants, and even politicians can choose from three paths.

PATH 1: Strive to apply the six growth leadership principles in our workplaces while ignoring, or worse, pretending to have rejected, the dark side of the protective mindsets. This option belongs to the strengths-based school of leadership and organizational development. It's the *comfortable* choice, but very vulnerable to the hypocrisy of "mindset washing." I call this the *optimistic* choice.

PATH 2: Accept the dark side and protective mindsets as the way the world works and learn to exploit people and resources, keep mining, and succeed in this world. People who get ahead in this way must live with, or not care about, the fact that their success validates a philosophy that restricts opportunity and franchise and harms others. This is an option that serves the few and keeps the majority where they are. I call this the *cynical* choice.

PATH 3: Forge a difficult and less trodden path that aspires to emulate the six growth principles, implement the bright side, and hold the dark side in check. This is the *courageous* choice.

If you've got this far in the book, you have what it takes to choose the third path. The self-important Hippos, sticky Snails, and tight-lipped Clams would have put it down long ago. I'm glad you're still here because we don't have much time and we need all the Dolphins we can find to join the growth mindset pod. We need to find each other, help others join the pod, and stick together.

Where to start?

As in *Star Wars,* there's no question that the dark side works for *some* people, those who want to achieve status, success, and monetary reward because of their Hippo-like behavior. They clearly don't want to change. I've also shown that Snails and Clams like things how they are (protected) and believe wholeheartedly in the success of their current mindset. All three will argue that to grow, somebody else or something else must change. We need new products, a new IT system, smarter people, or better leaders, they claim. Last on their list is a new mindset. Or is it?

In *Multipliers,* Liz Wiseman reflects on how people in her workshops respond unanimously "yes" to two questions: "How many of you would agree that the vast majority of the workforce possesses far more capability, creativity, talent, initiative, and resourcefulness than their present jobs allow or even require them to use?" and "Who here feels the pressure to produce more from less?" Her observation is that people are often "overworked and underutilized." Resolving this paradox is the key role of leadership: "Leadership is clearly a critical force for leveraging the full capability of the organization."

When people start to think about their own responses to change, high pressure, and uncertainty, they often begin to realize that they could benefit from better collaboration, clearer goals, and a bigger purpose. Mobilizing relational potential could make their job more impactful, a little easier, and more enjoyable. Even the Hippos I coach are stretched.

To start the journey to a growth mindset at an individual level, you need a why. Finding your why is about learning to see yourself and your relationships to the world differently. We're connected to each other emotionally, behaviorally, and physically (we share the planet). We can't solve big problems flying solo. We can't solve stress and burnout working more alone. Realizing these connections and the need to collaborate is a subtle but crucial step toward a growth mindset. For John, it was the Growth Mindset Leadership 360 assessment. For you, it could be reading this book.

At the organizational level, the journey to growth mindset starts with accepting the huge role leaders play in shaping whether their employees' mindsets grow or un-grow. Senior leaders not only set the tone and enable personal and team growth but also shape entire cultures. Satya Nadella inspired others to learn and grow. His leadership philosophy and practices have played a major role in refreshing Microsoft. Jack Welch inspired people to exploit and out-compete each other, to un-grow. He made shareholders rich but did so by outsourcing and offshoring whole industries, essentially ending manufacturing in the USA.

Welch's brand of leadership has infiltrated many organizations and perhaps even an entire nation. But I believe that

Welchian psychologies of leadership have reached their nadir. I believe we're beyond the point where hyper-individualized, hero-worshipping, power-hungry leadership practices create even the guise of prosperity.

My hope is that Nadella's philosophy becomes best in class in the coming years. In fact, it's my mission to help that happen.

After many years of mining the planet and our people for their resources and talents, we're facing a global catastrophe that demands a shift in mindset, culture, business models, and social practices. We need to stop mining and start growing human talent and potential.

I'm not expecting everyone to agree with me, at least not yet. And that's okay. Right now, we need a powerful coalition of first-movers and early adopters who are addicted to growth and demonstrate that you can be cool with a growth mindset and that important successful people adhere consistently to growth mindset principles. We need both empirical and social proof.

The transition from safe to great is challenging and uncomfortable. Part of this stems from the cognitive dissonance of having to hold in mind two contrasting views of the world, the bright and dark sides, and finding a path forward that brings them together. Here are four suggestions:

1. Be hopeful and determined about implementing the bright side.
2. Be more critical of and determined to reduce the dark side.
3. Drop the corporate BS that perpetuates cynicism and hypocrisy. Speak the truth.
4. Confront the biases that keep new and different people from participating in our teams and organizations.

16

The Conversation Continues

The typical story has three acts that go something
like this: The first act tells the audience what the problem is
and why they should care. The second act is where it
all goes wrong—so very, very wrong. The third act is where,
unlike in real life, it all gets resolved. How exactly
it ends, though, is, just like in real life, always a surprise.

ED CATMULL, Foreword to *Humour, Seriously*
by Jennifer Aaker and Naomi Bagdonas

In the preceding pages, I presented the constituent elements
of the Safe2Great model and some of the efforts needed to nurture great teams and organizations. I shared my dreams and
ambitions, as well as research revealing the positive effects
of a leadership philosophy based on psychological safety and
growth mindset. But the research and the story don't end here.
My intention, therefore, is to publish a series of books elabo-
rating on how we lead to succeed in the Green, Globotic, Caring, and Digital Enlightenment Ages.

Where this book has largely focused on leadership development and the theory and practice underpinning the Safe2Great model, my next book will consider the trajectory that takes us from Great to Green. How can we tackle the big issues of the Green Age? How can we deliver on zero-carbon initiatives and other programs vital to the longevity of the planet and humankind?

Since its inception, the aim of the Safe2Great project has been to build a case for making people, teams, and organizations self-transforming by adopting a growth mindset. Great teams, great organizations, and great civilizations grow because all their people grow, thriving rather than merely surviving.

I don't pretend to have all the answers. In this sense, this book and its planned sequels are an invitation to explore and develop the topic. This section doesn't offer resolution as such, but a willingness to hold uncertainty and adapt to it, continuing to question and explore.

I propose leaving you, therefore, not with pithy words to close out my thesis, but with the questions that have shaped this book and that I hope will encourage ongoing exploration of growth mindset and leadership.

Why do we need a growth mindset?

How can we create a self-motivating system that encourages high quality, excellence, and collaboration without using control or coercion?

How can we make the work we do and the changes we make more meaningful, contextualizing them in relation to our shared future?

How can we liberate our colleagues while still providing them with a sense of direction and fulfillment?

How can we foster open, playful, and questioning work relationships that challenge bias and established practice?

How can demonstrations of compassion and care inspire, energize, and strengthen the people we lead?

How can we persuade people to learn and change when it's against human nature to take risks?

How can we achieve alignment within and between teams, fostering supportive relationships that are about safety and respect rather than status and privilege?

Why are the growth mindset principles so uncommon in teams and organizations?

What happens when competition and control are the dominant leadership characteristics that shape organizational culture?

What happens when compliance and complacency are the dominant leadership characteristics that shape organizational culture?

What happens when criticism and skepticism are the dominant leadership characteristics that shape organizational culture?

What is the impact of controlling, compliant, and critical behaviors?

How do we shift from playing it safe to playing for great?

How do we play for great as individuals, teams, organizations, and societies, harnessing both personal and relational potential?

Do you have a growth mindset?

How do you know?

What purpose will it serve?

Bibliography

Aaker, Jennifer, and Naomi Bagdonas. *Humour, Seriously: Why Humour Is a Superpower at Work and In Life—and How Anyone Can Harness It, Even You.* Penguin, 2020.

Afeyan, Noubar, and Gary P. Pisano. "What Evolution Can Teach Us About Innovation." *Harvard Business Review* (September-October 2021). https://hbr.org/2021/09/what-evolution-can-teach-us-about-innovation

Albergotti, Reed, and Vanessa O'Connell. *Wheelmen: Lance Armstrong, the Tour de France, and the Greatest Sports Conspiracy Ever.* Gotham Books, 2013.

Almeida, Denise, Konstantin Shmarko, and Elizabeth Lomas. "The Ethics of Facial Recognition Technologies, Surveillance, and Accountability in an Age of Artificial Intelligence: A Comparative Analysis of US, EU, and UK Regulatory Frameworks." *AI and Ethics* 2, no. 1. (August 2022).

Amabile, Teresa, and Steven Kramer. *The Progress Principle: Using Small Wins to Ignite Joy, Engagement, and Creativity at Work.* Harvard Business Review Press, 2011.

Anderson, Lars. *A Season in the Sun: The Inside Story of Bruce Arians, Tom Brady, and the Making of a Champion.* William Morrow, 2021.

Anderson, Robert J., and William A. Adams. *Mastering Leadership: An Integrated Framework for Breakthrough Performance and Extraordinary Business Results*. Wiley, 2016.

Ansar, Atif, and Bent Flyvbjerg. "How to Solve Big Problems: Bespoke Versus Platform Strategies." *Oxford Review of Economic Policy* 38, no. 2 (2022): 338-68.

Arbinger Institute. *Leadership and Self-Deception: Getting Out of the Box*. Berrett-Koehler, 2018, third edition.

Baldwin, Richard. *The Globotics Upheaval: Globalization, Robotics, and the Future of Work*. Oxford University Press, 2019.

Berger, Jonah. *Contagious: Why Things Catch On*. Simon & Schuster, 2013.

Berger, Warren. *A More Beautiful Question: The Power of Inquiry to Spark Breakthrough Ideas*. Bloomsbury, 2018.

Black, J. Stewart, and Hal B. Gregersen. *It Starts with One: Changing Individuals Changes Organizations*. Wharton School Publishing, 2008, second edition.

Blackwell, Geoff. *Jacinda Ardern: I Know This To Be True—On Kindness, Empathy and Strength*. Chronicle Books, 2020.

Botsman, Rachel. *Who Can You Trust? How Technology Brought Us Together and Why It Could Drive Us Apart*. Portfolio Penguin, 2017.

Brenegar, Ed. *Circle of Impact: Taking Personal Initiative to Ignite Change*. Savio Republic, 2018.

British Academy. *Reforming Business for the 21st Century: A Framework for the Future of the Corporation*. The British Academy, 2018. https://www.thebritishacademy.ac.uk/publications/reforming-business-21st-century-framework-future-corporation/

Brown, William S. *Surveys of Organizational Culture and Safety Culture in Nuclear Power*. US Department of Energy, Office of Scientific and Technical Information, 2000. https://www.bnl.gov/isd/documents/20838.pdf

Bump, Jesse B., Peter Friberg, and David R. Harper. "International Collaboration and Covid-19: What Are We Doing and Where Are We Going?" *British Medical Journal* 372 (January 2021). https://www.bmj.com/content/372/bmj.n180

Camfield, David. *Future on Fire: Capitalism and the Politics of Climate Change*. PM Press, 2023.

Carney, Brian M., and Isaac Getz. *Freedom, Inc.: How Corporate Liberation Unleashes Employee Potential and Business Performance*. Somme Valley House, 2016, second edition.

Carson, Rachel. *Silent Spring*. Houghton Mifflin Company, 1962.

Catmull, Ed. "How Pixar Fosters Collective Creativity." *Harvard Business Review* (September 2008). https://hbr.org/2008/09/how-pixar-fosters-collective-creativity

Catmull, Ed, with Amy Wallace. *Creativity, Inc.: Overcoming the Unseen Forces That Stand in the Way of True Inspiration*. Bantam Press, 2014.

Clayton, Sarah Jensen, Tiernay Remick, and Evelyn Orr. "Today's CEOs Don't Just Lead Companies. They Lead Ecosystems." *Harvard Business Review* (June 9, 2022). https://hbr.org/2022/06/todays-ceos-dont-just-lead-companies-they-lead-ecosystems

Collins, Jim. *Good to Great: Why Some Companies Make the Leap— and Others Don't*. Harper Business, 2001.

Coyle, Daniel. *The Culture Code: The Secrets of Highly Successful Groups*. Bantam Books, 2018.

CPP, Inc. *Workplace Conflict and How Businesses Can Harness It to Thrive*. CPP Global Human Capital Report, July 2008.

Cross, R., R. Rebele, and A. Grant. "Collaborative Overload." *Harvard Business Review* (January-February 2016): 74-79. https://hbr.org/2016/01/collaborative-overload

Delizonna, Laura. "High-Performing Teams Need Psychological Safety: Here's How to Create It." *Harvard Business Review* (August 24, 2017). https://hbr.org/2017/08/high-performing-teams-need-psychological-safety-heres-how-to-create-it

Department of Economic and Social Affairs. *World Population Ageing 2019: Highlights*. United Nations, 2019. https://www.un.org/en/development/desa/population/publications/pdf/ageing/WorldPopulationAgeing2019-Highlights.pdf

Dewar, Carolyn, and Scott Keller. "The Irrational Side of Change Management." *McKinsey & Company* (April 1, 2009). https://www.mckinsey.com/capabilities/people-and-organizational-performance/our-insights/the-irrational-side-of-change-management

Diplomatic Rebels. *Transforming Organizations from Within.* http://www.diplomaticrebels.com/#story

Dowd, Maureen. "Lady of the Rings: Jacinda Rules." *New York Times* (September 8, 2018). https://www.nytimes.com/2018/09/08/opinion/sunday/jacinda-ardern-new-zealand-prime-minister.html

Duckworth, Angela. *Grit: The Power of Passion and Perseverance.* Vermilion, 2016.

Duhigg, Charles. *The Power of Habit.* Penguin, 2022, Kindle edition.

Dweck, Carol. *Mindset: Changing the Way You Think to Fulfil Your Potential.* Robinson, 2017, revised edition. Originally published as *Mindset: The New Psychology of Success,* 2006.

Edmondson, Amy C. *The Fearless Organization: Creating Psychological Safety in the Workplace for Learning Innovation and Growth.* Wiley, 2019.

———. *Teaming: How Organizations Learn, Innovate, and Compete in the Knowledge Economy.* Wiley, 2012, Kindle edition.

Eichenwald, Kurt. "Microsoft's Lost Decade." *Vanity Fair* (August 2012). https://www.vanityfair.com/news/business/2012/08/microsoft-lost-mojo-steve-ballmer

Ewing, Jack. *Faster, Higher, Farther: The Volkswagen Scandal.* W. W. Norton & Company, 2017, Kindle edition.

Foucault, M. *Discipline and Punish: The Birth of the Prison.* Translated by Alan Sheridan. Vintage Books, 1977.

Fromm, E. *Escape from Freedom.* Henry Holt and Company, 1941.

Gawande, Atul. *The Checklist Manifesto: How to Get Things Right.* Profile Books, 2011.

Gelles, David. *The Man Who Broke Capitalism: How Jack Welch Gutted the Heartland and Crushed the Soul of Corporate America— and How to Undo His Legacy.* Simon & Schuster, 2022, Kindle edition.

Goleman, Daniel. *Focus: The Hidden Driver of Excellence.* HarperCollins, 2013.

———. "What People (Still) Get Wrong About Emotional Intelligence." *Harvard Business Review* (December 22, 2020).

https://hbr.org/2020/12/what-people-still-get-wrong-about-emotional-intelligence

Grant, A. [@AdamMGrant]. "'That's my opinion and I'm sticking to it' is a self-limiting way to live. People who never let go of their views never evolve." Twitter, September 2, 2022. https://twitter.com/AdamMGrant/status/1565730168261443587

Gratton, Lynda. *Hot Spots: Why Some Companies Buzz with Energy and Innovation—and Others Don't*. Prentice Hall, 2007.

Gulati, Ranjay. *Deep Purpose*. HarperCollins, 2022, Kindle edition.

Gulati, R., C. Casto, and C. Krontiris. "How the Other Fukushima Plant Survived." *Harvard Business Review* 90, no. 5 (2012): 111-15.

Hansen, Morten T. *Collaboration: How Leaders Avoid the Traps, Create Unity, and Reap Big Results*. Harvard Business Press, 2009.

Hess, Edward D., and Katherine Ludwig. *Humility is the New Smart: Rethinking Human Excellence in the Smart Machine Age*. Berrett-Koehler, 2017.

Jacobides, Michael G. "In the Ecosystem Economy, What's Your Strategy?" *Harvard Business Review* (September-October 2019). https://hbr.org/2019/09/in-the-ecosystem-economy-whats-your-strategy

John Templeton Foundation. *Intellectual Humility*. https://www.templeton.org/discoveries/intellectual-humility

Kanter, Rosabeth Moss. "How Great Companies Think Differently." *Harvard Business Review* (November 2011). https://hbr.org/2011/11/how-great-companies-think-differently

——. "Ten Reasons People Resist Change." *Harvard Business Review* (September 25, 2012). https://hbr.org/2012/09/ten-reasons-people-resist-chang

Kegan, Robert, and Lisa Laskow Lahey. *Immunity to Change: How to Overcome It and Unlock the Potential in Yourself and Your Organization*. Harvard Business Press, 2009.

Kets de Vries, Manfred F. R. *The Leadership Mystique: Leading Behavior in the Human Enterprise*. Financial Times/Prentice Hall, 2006, second edition.

——. "Living in a Psychotic Age." INSEAD Working Paper No. 2022/50/EFE.

Kituyi, Mukhisa. "Covid-19: Collaboration is the Engine of Global Science—Especially for Developing Countries." *World Economic Forum* (May 15, 2020). https://www.weforum.org/agenda/2020/05/global-science-collaboration-open-source-covid-19/

Kohlrieser, George, with Susan Goldsworthy and Duncan Coombe. *Care to Dare: Unleashing Astonishing Potential Through Secure Base Leadership.* Jossey-Bass, 2012.

Kolisi, Siya, with Boris Starling. *Rise.* HarperCollins, 2021.

Kolisi Foundation. https://kolisifoundation.org

Kotter, John P. *Accelerate: Building Strategic Agility for a Faster-Moving World.* Harvard Business Review Press, 2014.

——. *Leading Change.* Harvard Business School Press, 1996.

Lencioni, Patrick. *Death by Meeting: A Leadership Fable . . . About Solving the Most Painful Problem in Business.* Jossey-Bass, 2004.

MacKenzie, Gordon. *Orbiting the Giant Hairball: A Corporate Fool's Guide to Surviving with Grace.* Viking, 1998.

Macur, Juliet. *Cycle of Lies: The Fall of Lance Armstrong.* William Collins, 2014.

Maslow, Abraham H. *The Psychology of Science: A Reconnaissance.* Zorba Press, 2002.

Massachusetts Institute of Technology. "Recalling the 'Giant Leap.'" *MIT News* (July 17, 2019). https://news.mit.edu/2009/apollo-vign-0717

McMillan, Robert. "Her Code Got Humans on the Moon—and Invented Software Itself." *Wired* (October 13, 2015). https://www.wired.com/2015/10/margaret-hamilton-nasa-apollo/

Microsoft. "Hybrid Work Is Just Work. Are We Doing It Wrong?" Microsoft WorkLab, 2022. https://www.microsoft.com/en-us/worklab/work-trend-index/hybrid-work-is-just-work

Mulhern, Owen. "Assessing Policy: The Montreal Protocol." *Earth.org.* September 28, 2020. https://earth.org/data_visualization/assessing-policy-the-montreal-protocol/#:~:text=The%20Former%20United%20Nations%20Secretary,to%20date"%20of%20any%20kind

Nadella, Satya, with Greg Shaw and Jill Tracie Nichols. *Hit Refresh: The Quest to Rediscover Microsoft's Soul and Imagine a Better Future for Everyone.* Harper Business, 2017.

National Institute of Mental Health. "Mental Illness." https://
www.nimh.nih.gov/health/statistics/mental-illness

Novo Nordisk. "Defeat Diabetes." https://www.novonordisk.com/
about/defeat-diabetes.html#

O'Connor, S., R. Campbell, H. Cortez, and T. Knowles. *Whale
Watching Worldwide: Tourism Numbers, Expenditures and
Expanding Economic Benefits*. International Fund for Animal
Welfare, 2009.

Patterson, Kerry, Joseph Grenny, Ron McMillan, and Al Switzler.
Crucial Conversations: Tools for Talking When Stakes Are High.
McGraw-Hill, 2012, second edition.

Pfeffer, Jeffrey. *7 Rules of Power: Surprising—but True—Advice on
How to Get Things Done and Advance Your Career*. Matt Holt
Books, 2022.

Pink, D. H. *Drive: The Surprising Truth About What Motivates Us*.
Riverhead Books, 2009.

Pontefract, Dan. *The Purpose Effect: Building Meaning in Yourself,
Your Role, and Your Organization*. Elevate, 2016.

Porath, Christine. "The Leadership Behavior That's Most Important
to Employees." *Harvard Business Review* (May 11, 2015).
https://hbr.org/2015/05/the-leadership-behavior-thats-most-
important-to-employees

———. *Mastering Civility: A Manifesto for the Workplace*. Balance, 2016.

———. *Mastering Community: The Surprising Ways Coming Together
Moves Us from Surviving to Thriving*. Balance, 2022.

———. "Why being respectful to your coworkers is good for business."
TED talk, October 2018. https://www.youtube.com/watch?v=
YY1ERM-NIBY

Pressfield, Steven. *The War of Art: Break Through the Blocks and
Win Your Inner Creative Battles*. Warner Books, 2002.

Queirós, Diego. "The Dark Age of Social Media." *Medium*. May 3,
2019. https://medium.com/@DiegoQueiros/the-dark-age-of-
social-media-f5b09043355c

Rao, Hayagreeva, Robert Sutton, and Allen P. Webb. "Innovation
Lessons from Pixar: An Interview with Oscar-winning Director
Brad Bird." *McKinsey Quarterly* (April 2008). https://www.
mckinsey.com/business-functions/strategy-and-corporate-

finance/our-insights/innovation-lessons-from-pixar-an-
interview-with-oscar-winning-director-brad-bird

Rogers, Carl R., and H. Jerome Freiberg. *Freedom to Learn*. Merrill, 1994, third edition.

Rushkoff, Douglas. *Team Human*. W. W. Norton, 2019.

Sandry, Richard, and Peter Urwin. *Estimating the Costs of Workplace Conflict*. Acas, May 2021. https://www.acas.org.uk/estimating-the-costs-of-workplace-conflict-report#foreword

Seppälä, Emma, and Kim Cameron. "Proof That Positive Work Cultures Are More Productive." *Harvard Business Review* (December 1, 2015). https://hbr.org/2015/12/proof-that-positive-work-cultures-are-more-productive

Simon, Herbert. "Designing Organizations for an Information-Rich World." In M. Greenberger (Ed.), *Computers, Communications, and the Public Interest*. Johns Hopkins Press, 1971.

Sloman, Steven, and Philip Fernbach. *The Knowledge Illusion: Why We Never Think Alone*. Penguin Publishing Group, 2015, Kindle edition.

Society for Human Resource Management. *SHRM Workplace Conflict Survey* (2017). https://www.shrm.org/hr-today/trends-and-forecasting/research-and-surveys/Documents/SHRM%20Workplace%20Conflict%20Survey%20Report.pdf

Sull, Donald, and Charles Sull. "How to Fix a Toxic Culture." *MIT Sloan Management Review* (September 28, 2022). https://sloanreview.mit.edu/article/how-to-fix-a-toxic-culture/

Sull, Donald, Charles Sull, William Cipolli, and Caio Brighenti. "Why Every Leader Needs to Worry About Toxic Culture." *MIT Sloan Management Review* (March 16, 2022). https://sloanreview.mit.edu/article/why-every-leader-needs-to-worry-about-toxic-culture/

Sutton, Robert. *The Asshole Survival Guide: How to Deal with People Who Treat You Like Dirt*. Houghton Mifflin Harcourt, 2017.

——. *Good Boss, Bad Boss: How to Be the Best—and Learn from the Worst*. Business Plus, 2012.

——. *The No Asshole Rule: Building a Civilized Workplace and Surviving One That Isn't*. Business Plus, 2007.

Tabrizi, Behnam. "How Microsoft Became Innovative Again."
Harvard Business Review (February 20, 2023). https://hbr.org/
2023/02/how-microsoft-became-innovative-again?ab=hero-
main-text

Thunberg, Greta. *No One Is Too Small to Make a Difference.*
Penguin, 2019.

Thunberg, Greta, Svante Thunberg, Malena Ernman, and Beata
Ernman. *Our House Is on Fire: Scenes of a Family and a Planet in
Crisis.* Translated by Paul Norlen and Saskia Vogel. Penguin,
2020.

Topol, Eric. *Deep Medicine: How Artificial Intelligence Can Make
Healthcare Human Again.* Basic Books, 2019, Kindle edition.

Twenge, Jean M., A. Bell Cooper, Thomas E. Joiner, Mary E. Duffy,
and Sarah G. Binau. "Age, Period, and Cohort Trends in Mood
Disorder Indicators and Suicide-Related Outcomes in a Nation-
ally Representative Dataset, 2005-2017." *Journal of Abnormal
Psychology* 128, no. 3 (2019). https://www.apa.org/pubs/
journals/releases/abn-abn0000410.pdf

UN Environment Programme. "Era of Leaded Petrol Over, Eliminating a Major Threat to Human and Planetary Health." United
Nations. August 30, 2021. Press release. https://www.unep.org/
news-and-stories/press-release/era-leaded-petrol-over-
eliminating-major-threat-human-and-planetary

Wadhwa, Vivek, and Ismail Amla, with Alex Salkever. *From Incremental to Exponential: How Large Companies Can See the Future
and Rethink Innovation.* Berrett-Koehler Publishers, 2020.

Weick, Karl E. *Sensemaking in Organizations.* Sage Publications, 1995.

Weick, Karl E., and Karlene H. Roberts. "Collective Mind in Organizations: Heedful Interrelating on Flight Decks." *Administrative
Science Quarterly* 38 (1993): 357-81.

Wiseman, Liz. *Multipliers: How the Best Leaders Make Everyone
Smarter.* Harper Business, 2017, revised edition.

World Health Organization. "Burn-out an 'Occupational Phenomenon': International Classification of Diseases." https://www.
who.int/news/item/28-05-2019-burn-out-an-occupational-
phenomenon-international-classification-of-diseases

Acknowledgments

This book would never have been possible without the energy and we'll-make-it-work attitude of my wife, Stephanie Vogelius Bowman. We have been through so much together while writing this book over the past six years. The death of my dear mother, buying a house together, our wedding, COVID-19, the birth of our first child, the purchase of Manoir du Suquet in France, and the birth of our twin girls. It's an ongoing experiment in growth mindset, and I wouldn't have it any other way. To infinity and beyond, my love.

My thanks to Richard Martin, my developmental editor, who helped me turn 900 pages of notes, hundreds of blogs, hours of videos, and lots of ideas in my head into a book. I couldn't have achieved a final draft without his insights, skill, and good-humored support.

Many thanks to Lesley Cameron, my editor from Figure 1, who has pushed me and my writing to the limit. It made a huge difference to the quality of this book. And it made it funnier.

I would also like to acknowledge the Safe2Great (Global Mindset) team who over the past twelve years have made so many hours at work fun, inspiring, and meaningful. We really do make organizations safe for great work. I may not have always practiced what I preach, but I hope you can forgive me (or forget) when I was a Hippo.

Index

197776

D

Danfoss, 54
Delizonna, Laura, 10
Deming, W. Edwards, 145
Dewar, Carolyn, 167
Digital Enlightenment Age, 8-9, 159, 164
diminishers, 107-9
Diplomatic Rebels, 94-95
diversity, 48, 92, 96
Dolphins: about, 36-38, 98-99, 111, 149, 161, 179; awareness and, 170-71; Bazball and, 38-40; vs. control, 44; Microsoft and, 40-42; transformation into, 155, 156
Duckworth, Angela, 81
Duhigg, Charles, 23, 106, 107
Dweck, Carol, 16, 17, 26, 77

E

ecosystems, 29, 54-55, 62, 161, 162, 163
Edmondson, Amy, 10-11, 12, 95-96, 117
emotions: emotional engagement, 72, 91, 96; emotional inhibition, 139; emotional resilience, 81-84; setting emotional tone, 79. *See also* psychological safety
empathy, 41, 53, 96, 139, 145
encouragement, 89-90
Ewing, Jack, 12
Explore, 71-77; about, 25, 71-72, 98; benefits, 73;

curiosity and, 75-76; guidance for, 77; Pixar's story, 73-75, 76-77

F

façades, 126-27
fear, 11, 12, 114, 117
Fernbach, Philip, 15
Foucault, Michel, 47
Fredrickson, Barbara, 10
freedom, 45, 68-69. *See also* autonomy
Friberg, Peter, 93
Fromm, Erich, 68
Fukushima Daini Nuclear Power Plant (Japan), 82-83

G

Gandhi, Mahatma, 165
GE, 121-22, 123
Gelles, David, 121, 122, 146-47
Globotic Age, 7, 55-56, 159, 160, 163. *See also* AI
GN ReSound, 48-49
Go High, 78-84; about, 25, 78-79, 99; benefits, 79; Christchurch mosque shootings and, 80-81; grit and, 81-84; guidance for, 84
Grant, Adam, 14, 156
Gratton, Lynda, 24, 48, 49, 61-62
Green Age, 5, 53-54, 62, 163, 183. *See also* climate change
Gregersen, Hal, 177
Grenny, Joseph, 11
grit, 81-84

growth mindset: about, 26-29,
30-31, 98-100, 159, 160-62;
acceleration and, 166,
175-76; acceptance and,
166, 171-73; action and, 166,
173-75; awareness and, 166,
167-71; implementation,
100, 149, 164-66, 178-79,
180-81; misunderstandings,
152; questions to consider,
183-84; safety inspectors
and, 35-36; Tiger Woods's
story, 177-78; Tom Brady's
story, 27-28. *See also* Aim
High; commitment; Dol-
phins; Explore; Go High;
Lift Others Up; Team Up;
Transform
Gulati, Ranjay, 62, 82-83

H

Hamilton, Margaret, 66-68, 69
Hansen, Morten, 95
Harper, David, 93
health care, 8, 52-53, 94, 144,
148-49, 161
hearing aids, 48-49
Hess, Edward, 6
High Reliability Organizations
(HROs), 50, 161
Hippos, 113-23; about, 110-11,
112, 113-14, 152, 162, 179;
anger and, 115-17; aware-
ness and, 169-70; blame
and, 117-19; consequences
of, 122-23; hippo-critical
organizations, 152; hybrid

work and, 150-51; men-
tal health impacts, 148;
No Hippo Zone, 153-54,
162-63; as pantomime
of power, 119-22, 168;
rule-breaking and, 120;
Snails and, 125, 131, 155-56;
traits, 115; transformation
into Dolphins, 155. *See also*
controlling leadership; protective mindsets
hot spots, 48-49, 61-62,
92, 161
humility, 18-19
humor, 72, 110, 154
Hurst, Aaron, 63

I

IBM, 8
illegality, 146-47
innovation, 10-11, 42-43, 44,
45, 48-49, 94-95
insecurity, 137-38

J

Jacobides, Michael, 54-55
Jobs, Steve, 45, 73, 75
journaling, 172-73
JPMorgan Chase, 8
just transition, 7, 160

K

Kanter, Rosabeth Moss, 85, 92
Kegan, Robert, 140
Keller, Scott, 167
Kets de Vries, Manfred F. R.,
11, 133

There wasn't enough room in this book to explain how to put the principles to work in your leadership and organization, so I've created free resources on my website to help you start your own Safe to Great journey.

Visit https://safe2great.com/bookclub to find:

· A summary of key points from each chapter

· Worksheets, challenges, and other exercises to help you implement the strategies discussed in this book

· A place to sign up for my newsletter, where I share ideas and further resources on developing psychological safety and a growth mindset

· Special offers on Safe2Great tools and online programs.

Printed in the USA
CPSIA information can be obtained
at www.ICGtesting.com
BVHW041856180823
668716BV00009B/49/J